CHRONICLES OF THE RAJ

CHRONICLES OF THE RAJ

*A Study of Literary Reaction to
the Imperial Idea towards
the End of the Raj*

SHAMSUL ISLAM

ROWMAN AND LITTLEFIELD

TOTOWA, NEW JERSEY

First published in the United States 1979
by Rowman and Littlefield, Totowa, N.J.

Library of Congress Cataloging in Publication Data

Shamsul Islam, 1942–
    Chronicles of the Raj.

    Bibliography: p.
    1. English literature—19th century—History and
criticism.   2. English literature—20th century—
History and criticism.   3. India in literature.
4. India—History—British occupation, 1765–1947.
I. Title.
PR469.I53S5   820'.9'3   79–12035
ISBN 0–8476–6174–1

Printed in Great Britain

TO AYESHA

who nearly ate the manuscript

Contents

Abbreviations

RUDYARD KIPLING

  DE   *Rudyard Kipling's Verse*, 'Definitive Edition'

E. M. FORSTER

  AH   *Abinger Harvest*
  HD   *The Hill of Devi*
  PI   *A Passage to India*
  TC   *Two Cheers for Democracy*

E. J. THOMPSON

  EI   *Enlist India for Freedom!*
  FI   *A Farewell to India*
  LI   *A Letter from India*
  RI   *The Reconstruction of India*

GEORGE ORWELL

  BD   *Burmese Days*
  RW   *The Road to Wigan Pier*

JOHN MASTERS

  BJ   *Bhowani Junction*
  BT   *Bugles and a Tiger*
  NB   *Nightrunners of Bengal*
  RM   *The Road Past Mandalay*

Acknowledgements

I wish to express my deep sense of gratitude to Professor Alan Heuser of the English Department at McGill University for going through the typescript and for many sessions of long and patient discussion on the subject. Although, because of my own limitations, I could not incorporate all the suggestions made by Professor Heuser, I remain beholden to him for valuable advice and constructive criticism.

This study was made possible by the grant of a leave of absence by Panjab University, a simultaneous appointment at the Université de Montréal during 1976–7 and a later appointment at McGill University during 1977–8. In this respect I am particularly obliged to Professor William Kinsley, Chairman of the English Department at the Université de Montréal and Professor Peter Ohlin, Chairman of the English Department at McGill University.

I am very grateful to the Social Sciences and Humanities Research Council of Canada for the award of a generous grant that enabled me to examine specialised source material in England and the Indo-Pakistan sub-continent.

Among other institutions and persons who assisted me, I must mention the British Council, which did an excellent job by putting me in touch with certain scholars and institutions in Britain.

Professor J. M. S. Tompkins, the distinguished Kipling scholar, constantly urged me to go ahead with this project and thus avoid being 'a one-book man'. Professor A. P. Thornton of the History Department at Toronto University also encouraged me. Mr Philip Mason was most kind in agreeing to meet me though unfortunately in the end I could not include him in this study. Dr R. J. Bingle of the India Office Library was also very helpful in many ways. I remain beholden to all these persons.

The publishers and I wish to thank the following who have kindly given permission for the use of copyright material: Edward Arnold (Publishers) Ltd and Harcourt Brace Jovanovich Inc. for the extracts from *A Passage to India* by E. M. Forster; Ernest Benn Ltd for the extracts from *A Farewell to India* by E. J. Thompson; A. M. Heath &

Co. Ltd on behalf of Mrs Sonia Brownell Orwell and the Orwell Estate for the extracts from *The Road to Wigan Pier, Burmese Days and Collected Essays* by George Orwell, published by Martin Secker & Warburg Ltd.

If by some mischance I have failed to seek permission or acknowledge where I should have done so, I hope those concerned will accept my apologies.

S. I.

1 Introduction

THE IMPERIAL IDEA AND THE RAJ

The expansion of England around the globe, and particularly in India, constitutes an 'imperial' epoch when East and West met together. The nature of this meeting, involving millions of people completely alien to each other, over a considerable period of time, is more significant for an understanding of British imperialism and its impact than a mere historical or political account of events describing the Empire. For, after all, what imperialism really denotes is a relationship: specifically, the relationship of a ruling or controlling power to those under its dominion. The nature of such a relationship will define the peculiar imperial idea or theory which results in that relationship.[1] What were the terms on which Britain met India, or for that matter Asia or Africa? What was the imperial idea which impelled the British to build an empire? Was there a viable imperial philosophy dedicated to some higher cause? Or was imperialism simply a manifestation of national ego? Was there, indeed, any substance to the imperial idea? These are the basic questions which confront a student of the intellectual content of imperialism, and these questions essentially concern the mystique of imperialism.

The development of the imperial mystique usually occurs after the event, and this mystique may not necessarily reflect the values actually incorporated in the political structure it helps keep going. There is always bound to be a gap between theory and practice. This does not however make the theory irrelevant. What the Romans thought of their *imperium* was highly relevant – it was, among other things, an essential means of cementing the structure they built.[2]

Theories of imperialism range from poetic fantasies to an empirical account of some aspects of reality carrying a built-in reference to the general philosophy of the theorist. A believer in liberal philosophy will see imperialism as absolutely immoral, for it implies subordination to a hegemonial power. A student of Marx and Engels will interpret imperialism from an economic point of view as nothing but

1

a method of exploitation. Today the term imperialism is pejorative, though this was not always the case. The root idea of empire in ancient and medieval days was that of a federation of states, under a universal law and a hegemony, covering the entire known world; it was based on a philosophy of peace, order, discipline, and internationalism.[3] Till the turn of the present century, imperialism was seen by many, particularly the Europeans, in more or less similar terms, especially as a civilising mission. The British ideal of service was epitomised in Kipling's poem 'The White Man's Burden', the French proclaimed their *mission civilisatrice*; and even the Germans, who entered rather late in the scramble for colonies, offered their superior *Kultur* to the world. The missionary zeal to bring the word of God to heathen peoples played no less important a part in giving respectability to the term imperialism. And others found comfort in the theories of Charles Darwin to present a racist 'God's elect' concept as justification for imperialist policies. The range of these theories of imperialism is thus wide and varied.

While the British domination of Asia and Africa is a long history of economic plunder, lust and loot, it is also a fascinating story of the development of an imperial theory, an imperial idea, a mystique about imperialism. Many of the above-mentioned theories lie at the heart of the imperial idea that stirred the imagination of the British for almost three centuries. In order to understand the nature and background of this imperial idea one has to go back to prophetic writers like Carlyle and Ruskin; to romantic politicians like Disraeli, Rhodes, and Curzon; to historians like Seeley, Freeman, and Froude; and to poets and novelists like Henty, Kipling, and Buchan — they all fostered and propagated an ideal of empire. In the late Victorian era, many Englishmen held this imperial idea as their main creed — the idea being that it was the divine mission of the Anglo-Saxons to civilise the world; to bring Asians and Africans the boons, both spiritual and material, of a superior civilisation; to establish light, order, and law in the dark places.[4]

India provided a testing ground for many of these theories, though of course the Raj was not launched as a socio-cultural experiment. Until the end of the eighteenth century, India was plundered systematically — the Company considered the country as a vast estate or plantation, the profits of which were to be withdrawn from India and deposited in Britain.[5] From the time of the Hastings trial, however, coinciding with Britain's own moral reawakening, India became an object of interest and reforming zeal. The impact of this new approach to India culminated in the reformist rule of Lord Bentinck, 1828 to 1835, when a vigorous campaign was launched for the reconstruction of Indian society. Social evils such as *suttee, thuggee* and female infanticide were rooted out. Men like Thomas Macaulay and C. E. Trevelyan introduced educational policies designed to Christianise and Westernise Indians. India appealed not only to Evangelicals, but also to political and social reformers. 'There was an opportunity in India,' wrote James Mill, 'to which the history of the world presents not a parallel.'[6] India excited Bentham and Bishop Heber as well as James and John Stuart Mill.[7]

After the Mutiny (1857), a change came over British thinking about India; liberal hopes for democratisation and a radical transformation of India were dashed; from then on emphasis was placed on a permanent Raj strongly dedicated to all the myths of the imperial idea. The suppression of the Mutiny had proved the triumph of the Christian God against the evil pagan deities; of Western culture over the Indian. Evolutionary theory, with the notion of the survival of the fittest popularised by Darwin's *Origin of Species* (1859), bolstered the notion of racial superiority as felt by the British over the natives. A stream of novels written in English from 1870 to the First World War about exotic lands shows the deep influence of Darwinian anthropology. These forces, then, economics, religion, politics, biology, and literature, served to spread the imperial gospel. India was to be ruled and served; this was confirmed by racial, political, and religious theories that were, at least to the British, both sound and moral.

India, to the prophets and the publicists of imperialism, was thus much more than the scene of a unique experiment in the government of alien peoples. It was also the great storehouse of ideals and purpose which were given their fullest expression in the high rhetoric of Curzon:

> But let it be our ideal all the same. To fight for the right, to abhor the imperfect, the unjust, or the mean, to swerve neither to the right hand nor to the left, to care nothing for flattery or applause or odium or abuse — it is so easy to have any of them in India — never to let your enthusiasm be soured or your courage grow dim, but to remember that the Almighty has placed your hand on the greatest of His ploughs, in whose furrow the nations of the future are germinating and taking shape, to drive the blade a little forward in your time, and to feel that somewhere among these millions you have left a little justice or happiness or prosperity . . . a dawn of

intellectual enlightenment, or a stirring of duty, where it did not before exist – that is enough, that is the Englishman's justification in India.[8]

India was a visible proof that such beliefs could work; a surprising number of the British in India were conscious of an imperial mission and even Nehru admitted that there was 'something of a religious temper'[9] about the British attitude to India.

The imperial idea, however, suffered its first real jolt with the South African War (or Boer War) at the turn of the century. This war disillusioned even the most utopian, intellectual imperialists and destroyed for good the dream of an Empire dedicated to internationalism, liberalism, and humanitarianism. The attack on the imperial idea became increasingly serious with the approach of the First World War, and no further emotional support was lent by the British public to overtly imperial policies.[10] Post-Darwinian anthropological thinking led by Malinowski at the turn of the century also contributed to the difficulty of believing in the racial or cultural superiority of the European that was imbedded in the imperial idea.[11] Now an attempt to place others in a universal hierarchy, by such criteria as 'race', 'intelligence', 'degree of monotheism', or even 'technology', was abandoned in favour of a study of native culture and institutions and the functions these served in the total life of a society. So anthropologists began to study the institutions of other societies in their own right, however strange they might seem by the standard of the observer's society.

A new rise in nationalism, and the political and economic evolution of the times are also important causes of the failure of the imperial idea. The idea finally collapsed by the time we reach the Second World War – in the mid-twentieth century it was no longer possible to believe in that superiority of the white man and of European civilisation and other myths which were used to justify an imperial mission. The failure of the imperial idea was the essential cause of the dismantling of the Raj in 1947, which was quickly followed by the disintegration of the entire Empire.

KIPLING AND THE RAJ

The British connection with India inspired a vast body of literature, especially fiction, which deserves to be classified into a separate genre.

The number of works dealing with India in the late Victorian period when the Raj was at its zenith is unbelievably high.[12] However, the literary merit of this genre is slight, with the exception of the works of Rudyard Kipling, whose shadow looms over the entire late Victorian and early modern period. It is Kipling, and later E. M. Forster, who give depth and respectability to literature of the Raj.

Generally speaking, literature on the imperial theme (especially Anglo-Indian literature) made a significant contribution to the spread of the mythology of Empire. It fostered the imperial idea by creating and popularising a corresponding body of myths or stereotyped images of India that rationalised the mystique of the Raj. Often these fictional types or images were taken as real by the British at home, and they would try to act accordingly on their arrival in India. The person who was able to project and perpetuate this mythology of both India and the Raj most successfully was Kipling; it is to Kipling that, to the majority of the British, the general public consciousness of the Empire really dates back. I will now briefly examine some of the stock images of India that strengthened the Raj and the imperial idea with particular reference to Kipling.[13]

The most recurrent image of Indians that emerges from Anglo-Indian literature is that of a child, or rather 'half devil and half child' as Kipling puts it. As a corollary of this image, the native is seen as a creature of impulse or emotion lacking in self-discipline.[14] The Indian, Kipling declares, 'is as incapable as a child of understanding what authority means, or where is the danger of disobeying it'.[15] It is therefore quite understandable why the dying Orde, Kipling's ideal civil servant, keeps on referring to the fierce men of his district as children who can easily go astray: 'But you must be good men when I am not here. . . . I speak now true talk, for I am as it were already dead, my children, for though ye be strong men, ye are children.' (IV, 173) This image of a child-like race fitted nicely with the British self-image of a mature, rational, strong-willed leader or father figure who was needed to take care of the child. The task of looking after the child, in an age moulded by the public-school spirit, could not be performed without the help of the rod; hence the rationale for the use of force in keeping India within the Empire. The logical conclusion of this child-parent or child-guardian relationship was that, however unpleasant, the Englishman had the god-given duty to protect, lead, and govern the Indians:

Take up the White Man's burden
Send forth the best ye breed —
Go bind your sons to exile
To serve your captives' need;
To wait in heavy harness
On fluttered folk and wild—
Your new caught, sullen peoples,
Half devil and half child.

Take up the White Man's burden —
Have done with childish days —
The lightly proffered laurel,
The easy, ungrudged praise.
Comes now, to search your manhood
Through all the thankless years,
Cold-edged with dear-bought wisdom,
The judgement of your peers![16]

Despite the call to humility, service, and sacrifice to his compatriots (such as expressed in the above-quoted lines), Kipling's conviction about the British right to rule in India and his categorisation of mature and child-like races expose him to the charge of racism. It is true that he does see certain inherent virtues in Anglo-Saxon blood. For instance, an English child like Wee Willie Winkie can disperse a hostile horde of Pathans by an emphatic '*Jao*' (go) or even a Eurasian such as Michele d'Cruze can quell a riot simply because of a drop of English blood in his veins. Similarly, the notoriously offensive words 'lesser breeds without the Law' in his 'Recessional' have been taken as further proof of Kipling's racial bias. Nevertheless, as compared to his contemporaries, one must observe that Kipling, though proud of Anglo-Saxon achievements, does not degenerate into the kind of racial bigotry practised and preached by many others.[17] However, a race-consciousness is certainly there; but Kipling could not help going against this spirit of his times. Thus we see him advocating the desirability of keeping to one's race, caste, or creed: Englishmen who 'go native' in his works always suffer terribly, and love affairs between Englishmen and Indian girls in his tales always end tragically.

Anglo-Indian fiction abounds in the role of the native as a loyal sepoy or servant to the British; this too fits well with the basic conception of the native as a child — a master-servant relationship is just another extension of the guardian-child or parent-child relationship, especially in a rigid Victorian context. In a sense, as Louis Cornell remarks, the loyal and affectionate servant remained for Kipling the prototype of the admirable Indian native.[18] Kipling's stories are full of obedient Imam Dins and other *khidmatgars* of his type whom he or his protagonists could order about. In 'Tods' Amendment' the child Tods is described in these words:

> Tods was the idol of some eighty 'Jhampanis' and half as many 'saises'. He saluted them all as 'O Brother!' It never entered his head that any living human being could disobey his orders; and he was the buffer between the servants and his Mamma's wrath.
>
> (I, 218— 19)

In 'The Tomb of his Ancestors', John Chinn, whose grandfather had been associated with the Bhils, returns to his native regiment and is worshipped as a god:

> A faint light burned in his room and, as he entered, hands clasped his feet and a voice murmured from the floor . . . 'I bore you in my arms, Sahib, when I was a strong man and you were a small one — crying, crying, crying! I am your servant, as I was your father's before you. We are all your servants.'
>
> (XIII, 133— 4)

The belief in the childlike primitivism of Indians led the British to focus their attention on people who fitted closely with the stereotype, to the peasant cultivators and tribal groups or, at the other end of the scale, the decadent princes whom the British could patronise and encourage against an emerging urban middle-class intelligentsia. Hence the *ryot* (peasantry) and the *rajahs* who posed no threat to the Raj became the real Indians while the educated, especially Western-educated, natives were dismissed as hybrid, of no significance at all. Since the Bengalis led in education, it was the Bengali *babu* who came to be regarded as the representative hybrid Indian and became a stock figure of ridicule in Anglo-Indian literature.

Another common concept in Kipling and other writers on India is that of the inscrutable India. It is argued that the differences between Indians and the British are so wide that one can never bridge the gap:

You'll never plumb the Oriental mind,
And if you did it isn't worth the toil.
Think of a sleek French priest in Canada;
Divide by twenty half-breeds; multiply
By twice the Sphinx's silence. There's your East.
And you're as wise as ever. So am I.

(DE, 69–70)

This so-called inscrutability of the East lent a kind of legitimacy to the distance that the British kept from the natives and which later on came to be recognised as a prime cause of the estrangement between the two sides. Sometimes this lack of understanding was even given a philosophic justification, for India is seen as a separate entity embodying powers of darkness which defy comprehension and present a challenge to the forces of order or light. This becomes another argument for the acceptance of the imperial idea. Kipling's well-known story 'The Bridge Builders' presents such a view in a nutshell. The struggle between the spirit of India and modern civilisation is symbolised by a bridge-building over the Ganges that is no longer tolerated by Mother Gunga; she is only appeased when she is reminded that it is all *maya* anyway and that the spirit of India can never be vanquished. This view brings into relief the heroism of the upholder of the imperial idea who accepts the challenge of the dark powers in the face of heavy odds. Kipling's civil servants are thus engaged in a heroic struggle:

> Year by year England sends out fresh drafts for the first fighting-line, which is officially called the Indian Civil Service. These die, or kill themselves by overwork, or are worried to death, or broken in health and hope in order that the land may be protected from death and sickness, famine and war, and may eventually become capable of standing alone. It will never stand alone, but the idea is a pretty one, and men are willing to die for it, and yearly the work of pushing and coaxing and scolding the country into good living goes forward.

(IV, 305–6)

Kipling's tales in fact tell us more of the local problems of British administrators in keeping law and order in areas of darkness and chaos and of Indian daily life than of the public political situation of the time.

The 'good government' provided by the British is often contrasted with the corruption of the Indian princes or the bad rule of other imperial powers such as the Portuguese. The native states are 'the dark places of the earth, full of unimaginable cruelty, touching the railway and the telegraph on one side, and on the other, the days of Harun-al-Raschid.' (V, 44) A group of Kipling's efficient civil servants laugh at the attack on the Raj levelled by a visiting British MP; they justify their presence in India by citing the despotism and corruption of the native princes in reference to their harems:

> The darlings haven't had any new clothes for nearly a month, and the old man wants to buy a new drag from Calcutta – solid silver railings and silver lamps, and trifles of that kind. I've tried to make him understand that he played the deuce with the revenues for the last twenty years and must go slow. . . . I've known the taxman wait by a milch-camel till the foal was born and then hurry off the mother for arrears.
>
> (V, 332–3)

The extent to which the natives lack the ability to govern themselves is shown by the ease with which two ordinary English 'loafers' in 'The Man Who Would Be King' found a kingdom in Kafiristan, a remote area on the North West Frontier, and prove to be beneficent rulers for a while.[19]

The combined image of India as dark power and natives as children goes along with climatic theories about tropical or sub-tropical cultures and a negative view of Indian religions, especially Hinduism. Before Darwin, racial distinctness was usually considered the result either of separate divine creations or of the effect of climate over a period of time. In India it was the sinister climate which, for example, was seen as the cause of indolence, passivity, or even depravity of the natives which made them into an inferior race.[20] Similarly, native customs and faiths, particularly the Hindu, appalled the British; Hinduism confirmed their belief in the perverse and evil character of Indians – this was the only way they could understand *suttee*, child-marriage, caste, female infanticide, or idol worship. Kipling, however, did not go so far as to support the climatic theory. He did share a dislike of Hinduism, which went with a corresponding liking for Islam.[21] Kipling was no religious bigot; in fact he was quite critical of Christianity and came to respect all religions. His case against Hinduism was that it seemed to sanction most of India's social problems against which he and other upholders of the imperial idea were waging a war.

With this perspective of a child-like, changeless, and half-evil India, it was easy for Kipling or other Anglo-Indian writers of this period to pooh-pooh the nationalists. Nationalism was simply ignored or dismissed as not representative of real India. As Hutchins remarks, it is almost impossible to find references to nationalist politics in contemporary memoirs.[22] The comments of Edwards, an old friend of the visiting British MP Pagett in 'The Enlightenment of Pagett, M.P.' typify Kipling's view: 'There are no politics, in a manner of speaking, in India. It's all work'. (IV, 350) Edwards' statement is confirmed by the passionate rhetoric of Dr Eva McCreery Lathrop, chief of the Women's Hospital in Asmara: 'Well, what's wrong with this country is not in the least political, but an all-round entanglement of physical, social, and moral evils and corruptions, all more or less due to the unnatural treatment of women. . . . It's right here where the trouble is, and not in any political considerations whatsoever.' (IV, 380) Similarly, on his 1888 visit to Calcutta, a horrified Kipling worried about cleaning up the slums while the Indian councillors were busy discussing J. S. Mill and democratic values; he was again convinced of the irrelevance of democracy: 'Where is the criminal, and what is all this talk about abstractions? They want shovels, not sentiments, in this part of the world.'[23]

With this conviction about the need for practical work rather than political democracy went the general assumption that the nationalists were neither popular nor capable of running the country. Communal tension between Muslims and Hindus was used as another argument for the presence of an impartial British regime.[24] In fact, by this time (late 1880s) British aspirations in India had shifted from hope for total and quick reconstruction of the society to a view that Britain's mission in India was to 'keep law and order'.[25] A long essay by Kipling on the 1888 meeting of the Indian National Congress, then in its third year, leaves no doubt about his point of view. He ridicules the Congress by observing that they were incapable of conducting an orderly meeting, let alone the affairs of the sub-continent.[26] Often he is at pains to point out that the average Indian has not even heard of the Congress and that it does not represent large groups such as Muslims and Christians.[27] The two villains of the piece, Indian nationalism and British democracy, were thus joined together in a single argument. The nationalist agitator was seen as a naughty child who was spoilt by misguided British liberals and democrats who did not realise that Western ways could not work in the Orient.[28]

By the third quarter of the nineteenth century, Britain's imperial policy underwent a major change in the face of the new European and even American competitors; this made India more important to the Empire. It was now argued that Britain should rule India permanently; the combination of India, the white colonies, and Britain would produce a grand political structure which nobody could hope to surpass. This concept was first projected in two books – Charles Dilke's *Greater Britain* (1869) and J. R. Seeley's *The Expansion of England* (1883). The moral issue of subjugating India on a permanent basis was solved by denying her the status of a nation which was always accepted in the past.[29]

One can gather some impression of Britain's changing sense of her imperial destiny by the increasing parallels drawn to the ancient Roman Empire with particular reference to the Raj in India. This is a standard theme in the writings of James Mill, Macaulay, and C. E. Trevelyan. And Kipling wrote a number of stories about an imaginary Roman Britain which bore a greater resemblance to contemporary India. Here Kipling raises his imperial philosophy to its most philosophic level. Rome, standing for the imperial idea, builds the Wall wherever she goes even if not always in masonry. The Wall, symbolic of the Law, divides civilisation, however imperfect, from the barbarous and lawless world that lies outside the Wall.[30] The Wall is adorned with a statue of Roma Dea – symbolic of the relationship between the Law and the imperial idea. The Wall cannot exist without Rome though it is not just defended by Roman armies; it is guarded by many different nationalities. These soldiers, stationed in Britain, invoke the help of Rome:

> *Strong heart with triple armour bound*
> *Beat strongly, for Thy life-blood runs,*
> *Age after Age, the Empire round –*
> *In us Thy Sons,*
>
> *Who, distant from the Seven Hills,*
> *Loving and serving much, require*
> *Thee – Thee to guard 'gainst home-born ills*
> *The Imperial Fire!*

(XXIII, 163)

The Roman tales are significantly set at the time of the disintegration of the Empire; this confirms the analogy with the state of the
Raj in India. It has also been pointed out that Hadrian's Wall against
the Picts and the Winged Hats resembles the Khyber Pass on the
North West Frontier. The description of the Picts is highly suggestive
of Bengali nationalism:

> *We are the worm in the wood!*
> *We are the rot at the root!*
> *We are the germ in the blood!*
> *We are the thorn in the foot!*
>
> ('A Pict Song', XXIII, 223)

There is no question that the Roman tales are intended as parables of
the Raj in India. The significance of the Raj or Rome seems to reside
in the idea it embodies; although the Roman Empire is shown to be in
a state of disorder the imperial idea remains imperishable:[31] it
provides a structure of order and civilisation against disorder and
barbarity.

One must however note that Kipling's imperialism is counterbal-
anced by his love for India, which deeply informs his masterpiece
Kim — the finest English novel about India, as Nirad C. Chaudhuri
has put it. Here, although the framework is that of the imperial game
of espionage and counter-espionage, the main focus of the novel is on
the humanity, spirituality, and timelessness of India. The central
figure of this novel is no sabre-rattling Tommy or civil servant toiling
in the remote corners of the Empire; the real protagonist here is India
who reveals herself in diverse ways — in the never-ceasing hustle and
bustle of the Grand Trunk Road; in the saint-like person of Teshoo
Lama of Tibet who is in search of his River of the Arrow, where he
expects to find his *nirvana*; in the glamorous and masculine world of
Mahbub Ali, the Pathan horse-dealer of Lahore; and even in Kim, the
white-faced boy of Lahore who can pass for both Hindu and Muslim.
The theme of the novel is Kim's search for identity, which is closely
tied up with the Lama's quest for an annihilation of identity. Kim,
though he chooses the world of action represented by Mahbub Ali, is
more deeply influenced by the Search rather than the great Game: his
spiritual and moral awakening is the direct result of the Lama's gentle
influence. So *Kim* and Kipling's ambivalent attitude towards India
complicate matters; they tend to vitiate or at least seriously modify his
stereotyped images of India and the Raj.

AIM, SCOPE AND SIGNIFICANCE OF THIS STUDY

The literature on the imperial theme, particularly on the Raj, falls into two main groups in terms of its attitude to the imperial idea — one up to Kipling and the other post-Kipling. The first period can be designated as the Era of Confidence when the imperial mood was most widespread and the imperial idea was taken for granted. The second period begins with the First World War in 1914 when the confidence in the imperial idea was seriously shaken and the whole *raison d'être* of the Empire began to be questioned. The post-Kipling period may be termed the Era of Doubt and Melancholy; this period extends from 1914 to the present time. However 1947 may be taken as the real terminal year of this phase of doubt and melancholy for it marks the dismantling of the Raj in India, which was the mainstay of the Empire and the imperial idea for such a long time.

I am concerned with a study of the second phase roughly covering the period 1914–47 when the imperial idea was in decline; I am interested in examining the literary reaction to the imperial idea during this time. Did the English writers accept the changing attitude towards the Raj and the imperial idea? Did they recognise the moral and economic implications of colonisation? Did they sympathise with the national movements for liberation? Or did they try to hold on to the old imperial idea in an attempt to save the Empire? Or did they simply ignore the problem?

Out of a host of writers from this period, I have chosen four; E. M. Forster, Edward J. Thompson, George Orwell[32] and John Masters, for between them they represent the main forms of the literary reaction to the dying Raj. I should have liked to include others, particularly Philip Mason, but reasons of space do not allow this. I am also conscious of the fact that by concentrating on the Raj in India, I am excluding many important writers on the imperial theme working within the context of the Empire in Africa or elsewhere — for instance, Joyce Cary, Evelyn Waugh and Graham Greene. My main reason for doing so is that India offers the key to the understanding of British imperialism and the imperial idea in general, for the pattern of British colonial policy was formed in India; and to the British, Empire with all its romantic associations meant chiefly India. Secondly, India confronted the British with an older and more comprehensive civilisation than the one they brought with them and the question of the superiority of the Western civilisation confused and confounded anyone who cared to think. Africa or Australia or the West Indies presented no such problem to the empire-builder — there the civilising mission appeared to need no moral justification. It was in India that the imperial idea underwent a real challenge and a test; hence it is more interesting to see how sensitive English writers working within the context of the Raj reacted to the changing political, social, economic, and historical realities.

My point of reference throughout will be Kipling, who is the chief exponent of the imperial idea. One of the questions that I will be constantly raising is: 'Do these writers in the twentieth century accept the stereotyped images of India that are perpetuated by Kipling or not?' In other words, I will keep an eye on the degree of deviation or similarity of these writers' concepts of India and Indians from that of Kipling; this difference will be an indication of their reaction to the imperial idea and the Raj. My approach to the subject will however be basically historical.

I may point out that because of the vast differences in the calibre of writers under study and also because of the nature of my subject, the various sections of this book may seem to lack the uniformity and evenness that one expects in a book on a single topic. Despite such unevenness, the unity of the study is defined by its object — fictive reaction to the imperial idea at the end of the British Raj in India, 1914–47.

Finally, a question of the value of such an investigation may be raised. Apart from my personal interest, I believe that history and literature interact and illuminate each other. Often literature, though less objective and more emotional, is a better guide to the spirit of the times. There are many historical and political studies of the rise and fall of the imperial idea, but the subject has not received much literary attention though it inspired a vast body of literature. So this study is an attempt at filling this gap to a certain extent.[33] Moreover, although the Empire is dead and gone, it affected millions of people in an intimate way for centuries; it changed the course of present history; and the ideas which generated and later destroyed it continue to exercise their influence on our lives in ways that cannot be calculated — the whole question of East-West relationship or inter-personal and inter-racial communication, or the role of the Third World in the present scheme of things, has something to do with the imperial idea; this is what makes this investigation relevant today.[34]

2 E. M. Forster

We are all familiar with Forster's creed – liberal humanism and belief in personal relationships and the private life.[1] Forster's non-fiction leaves no doubt as to the centrality of political beliefs in his moral framework, and the novels reflect his deepest and most generalised thoughts on the subject. And so naturally literary historians (who are fond of neat classifications) tend to see him as an antithesis of all that Kipling and his school is supposed to have stood for, namely, jingo imperialism, white man's burden, and other reactionary myths perpetuating Western domination of the Third World.[2] While there is some truth in these generalisations, I believe that the relationship between Forster and Kipling is not one of simple inversion and that Kipling has been too harshly judged by his critics. One is often struck by similarities rather than contrasts between these two writers whose imaginations were stirred by the same source – India.[3] I will come to this theme in a later section, and all that I want to suggest here is that despite Forster's liberal and anti-imperial stance, one cannot understand his complex relationship to India and the imperial idea through linear formulae.

E. M. Forster died in 1970 at the age of 91, and his writing career spanned more than fifty years from the turn of the century onward. But his career as a novelist in fact falls into a shorter period, the period from around the century's turn until 1924, the year in which *A Passage to India* appeared.[4] *A Passage to India* is Forster's most explicit statement on the imperial idea and his views on the subject remained relatively unmodified by later experiences or writings. Thus this novel, along with another interesting book, *The Hill of Devi* (1953) – a collection of letters that Forster wrote during his stay in India – are most pertinent to this study.

A Passage to India and *The Hill of Devi* are the products of Forster's two visits to India in 1912–13 and 1921. He first set out for India on 7 October 1912 in the company of his friends Goldsworthy Lowes Dickinson and R. C. Trevelyan. At that time, as Forster tells us in his 'Indian Entries', he had no intention of writing a book on India – he went to sightsee and stay with friends, particularly with Syed Ross Masood, to whom he dedicated *A Passage to India*.[5]

Forster's friendship with Masood played a very significant role in the development of his mind and heart. He first met this handsome, cultured, emotional, and warm Indian Muslim, full of nostalgia for the glories of the Moghul past, around 1906 when he was hired to coach him in Latin. Soon the relationship with Masood turned into an affair of the heart — he awakened Forster out of his academic shell and showed him new horizons:

> My debt to him [Masood] is incalculable. He woke me up out of my suburban and academic life, showed me new horizons and a new civilization and helped me towards the understanding of a continent. Until I met him, India was a vague jumble of rajahs, sahibs, babus, and elephants, and I was not interested in such a jumble.
>
> (TC, 296)

It was in fact Masood who helped him formulate his theory of the developed heart, for Masood's ruling passion was friendship.[6]

Forster landed in Bombay on October 22 and headed straight for Aligarh to see Masood. He stayed with him for a week and was overwhelmed by the hospitality and warmth of his friend. In going to Aligarh, as pointed out by his biographer Furbank, Forster had unwittingly plunged himself into the thick of Indian politics, for at that time Aligarh was the centre of Muslim nationalism, particularly of the pan-Islamic Khilafat Movement spearheaded by the Ali Brothers.

Other significant experiences in India included his meetings with the 'fantastic and endearing' Maharajah of Chhatarpur to whom he had an introduction. The Maharajah's passion was philosophy and he heartily welcomed the learned Cambridge visitors, entertaining them with Hindu mystery plays, *nautches* (dances), elephant rides, and endless discussions on metaphysical problems. Forster next went to Indore where he met the youthful Maharajah of Dewas Senior, Sir Tukoji Rao III (known as Bapu Sahib) who, after Masood, was the next Indian to exercise the deepest influence on him. Forster returned to England in April 1913.[7]

Forster's second visit to India from April to November 1921 was in the capacity of private secretary to the Maharajah of Dewas Senior, an interlude of which he later wrote, 'It was the great opportunity of my life' when he was able to see 'so much of the side of life that is hidden from most English people'.[8] *The Hill of Devi* is a record of some of these insights into India. Forster's last visit to India was in 1945, when he came to attend the All India PEN Conference held at Jaipur – the visit was however a brief one.

A Passage to India was started and mostly written during Forster's 1912–13 visit though it was published twelve years later in 1924. And politically its framework is that of India before the First World War, which makes it a bit dated.[9] The political situation in India had undergone a great change since the First World War. The Indian National Congress was no longer limited to an intellectual coterie; the independence movement had taken hold of the imagination of all Indians down to the toiling *ryot* (peasantry) – the 'real Indians' as the English preferred to call them. Gandhi had launched his *satyagraha* (civil disobedience) movement in 1920, and things were no longer non-violent after the 1919 massacre of peaceful Indians by General Dyer at Jallianwallah Bagh in Amritsar.[10] The Moplah Rebellion took place on the Malabar Coast in August 1921, two years after the Amritsar massacre. The Khilafat Movement was at its peak during 1921–2 in which both Muslims and Hindus pressed the British government not to depose the Turkish Sultan after his defeat in the Great War. *A Passage to India* takes no note of these developments; it remains unmodified by the politics of the twenties and the same is true of *The Hill of Devi*, which is perhaps more backward-looking than the novel as it conjures up a rather romantic picture of the feudal, princely India.

It is therefore not surprising that the novel did not make much impact on Indian nationalists. 'The book', notes Natwar-Singh, 'failed to impress the Indian nationalists who consisted largely of middle-class intellectuals. It made little or no impact in India. The issues had gone beyond good manners. It succeeded in annoying the British without satisfying Indian political aspirations.'[11] Andrew Shonfield, in his article 'Politics of Forster's India', goes a step further and charges that 'Forster had little understanding and no sympathy for the complicated and courageous politics of Indian independence movement'.[12] Perhaps this is an extreme view and even Natwar-Singh does not agree with Shonfield on this score; he cites Forster's admiration for Indian leaders, especially Nehru and Tagore, as proof of his sympathy and understanding of the Indian scene.

The question of Forster's stand on India and the imperial idea is however not a simple one of acceptance or rejection of the Indian

National Congress and its leaders, as Natwar-Singh or Shonfield endeavour to show. To begin with, one must remember that Forster is not primarily interested in politics though *A Passage to India* has a political aspect. Natwar-Singh himself records Forster's response to the question of Indo-British reaction to the novel when it first appeared in 1924:

> It had some political influence — it caused people to think of the link between India and Britain and to doubt if that link was altogether of a healthy nature. The influence (political) was not intended; I was interested in the story and the characters. But I welcomed it.[13]

As a novelist it was not Forster's responsibility to propose political solutions to what he termed 'the tragic problem of India's political future'. (TC, 331) 'I do not know what political solution is correct,' (TC, 324) he wrote as late as 1946 (almost on the eve of independence) after his last visit to India. And this is precisely the position that Cyril Fielding, who is in many ways Forster's spokesman in *A Passage to India*, adopts whenever he is pressed by his Indian friends to express his views on the political issue. 'I cannot tell you why England is here or whether she ought to be here. It's beyond me,'[14] Fielding declares in a non-committal fashion.

The point I am trying to make is that politics is not Forster's main concern in *A Passage to India* or even *The Hill of Devi* though this does not imply that he was not aware of the complex political developments around him.[15] For after all *A Passage to India* is not a political treatise — it is a highly wrought work of art. And like all great writers, Forster here concerns himself with issues that go beyond the merely topical. Thus though the Indian political situation of the pre-1914 era is relevant to the novel, Forster, like his predecessor Kipling, is preoccupied with larger, more essential issues. I would suggest that the basic questions that Forster poses are:

> What is India (India as an entity separate from Indians)?
> Who are the real Indians (real in the sense as to who understand the reality of India and conform to the dictates of this reality)?
> What is the position and role of aliens such as the English in India?
> What is the nature of the relationship between Indians and the English?

It is in the context of the last question that the validity of the imperial idea is examined, for it is the Raj that brings Indians and the British together. The imperial or political theme is thus secondary to the philosophic theme. However, the first two questions concerning the reality of India are equally relevant to this study for here one sees Forster's essential vision of India that can help us determine the extent to which he differs from or conforms to the stereotyped images of India and its people.

THE MARABAR CAVES: FORSTER'S VISION OF INDIA

The central character of *A Passage to India*, like that of Kipling's Indian works, is 'the great, grey, formless India', to borrow Kipling's words. Forster, like Kipling, is both attracted and baffled by India, and his vision of India is not very different from that of Kipling. It is essentially a vision of chaos or at best an admission of one's utter failure to come to terms with India. The enigma of India, for both Forster and Kipling, remains unsolved – she is, to use another of Kipling's apt phrases, 'the great Sphinx of the Plains'.

India overwhelms and crushes one in every respect. Speaking to Mrs Hauksbee, the socialite of Kipling's Simla, Mrs Mallow remarks: 'Surely twelve Simla seasons ought to have taught you that you can't focus anything in India.'[16] Forster agrees with Kipling's view: 'Little is clear-cut in India,' he admits with dismay (HD, 39). This theme of a lack of clarity in India becomes a *leitmotiv* in *A Passage to India*. The most important image of India that emerges in the novel is that India is a muddle, a grand chaos that one can never plumb despite one's best efforts. 'A mystery is only a high-sounding term for a muddle,' Fielding explains and he goes on to say, 'Aziz and I know that India's a muddle.' (PI, 68)

India represents a plane of reality which cannot be classified or catalogued by the Western mind. This inscrutability of India, which is a common theme in most writings in English about India, is suggested repeatedly in the novel. At the polo match, for example, Adela notices a little greenish bird flying into the trees, and she wants Ronny to identify the bird, but Ronny cannot do so. Forster remarks: 'But nothing in India is identifiable, the mere asking of a question causes it to disappear or to merge in something else.' (PI, 83–4) At a later point as Aziz and the ladies reach the Marabar hills, Adela notices a thin, dark object on the far side of a watercourse, and exclaims: 'A snake!' The villagers and Aziz agree, but when Adela looks through Ronny's field-glasses, she discovers that it was not a snake, but a withered stump of a toddy-palm. So she says, 'It isn't a snake,' but the villagers contradict her, and even Aziz insists that it was a black cobra who looked like a tree through the glasses. 'Nothing was explained, and yet there was no romance,' Forster comments (PI, 139).

There is no single, well-defined pattern in India. This is the lesson that Mrs Moore learns as she sails home and the thousands of coconut palms on the coastline bid her farewell: '"So you thought an echo was India; you took the Marabar caves as final?" they laughed. "What have we in common with them, or they with Asirgarh? Good-bye!"' (PI, 205) India appears as a microcosm of 'the echoing contradictory world' (PI, 122) which cannot be grasped: 'India is the country, fields, fields, then hills, jungles, hills, and more fields. . . . How can the mind take hold of such a country?' Forster asks and goes on to say:

> Generations of invaders have tried, but they remain in exile. The important towns they build are only retreats, their quarrels the malaise of men who cannot find their way home. India knows of their trouble. She knows of the whole world's trouble, to its uttermost depth. She calls 'Come' through her hundred mouths, through objects ridiculous and august. But come to what? She has never defined. She is not a promise, only an appeal.
>
> (PI, 135)

India here assumes the metaphor for the unconscious and the irrational, an area of darkness which is at once terrifying and irresistible.

For Forster's most meaningful statement on his vision of India, one must turn to the superb description of the Marabar Caves that is so rich in symbolism. Forster begins by suggesting the unthinkable antiquity of the hills of Dravidia; they are contemporaneous with the beginning of creation, the time of the Genesis.

Next Forster takes us right to the caves which one finds difficult to discuss for 'nothing, nothing attaches to them, and their reputation — for they have one — does not depend upon human speech.' (PI, 124) The only way Forster can describe these caves is in terms that are abstract and negative, though not necessarily pejorative. One immediate thing that he notes is that the caves are dark and even when they open towards the sun, very little light penetrates inside. If one strikes a match in these caves, it only heightens their mystery and appeal instead of revealing their reality.

Moreover, the majority of the caves have never been opened up – 'chambers never unsealed since the arrival of the gods'. Here Forster clearly notes the pre-Hindu character of these caves, implying the powerlessness of Hinduism to completely comprehend the reality represented by them:

> Hinduism has scratched and plastered a few rocks, but the shrines are unfrequented, as if pilgrims, who generally seek the extra-ordinary, had here found too much of it. Some saddhus did once settle in a cave, but they were smoked out, and even Buddha, who must have passed this way down to the Bo Tree of Gya, shunned a renunciation more complete than his own, and has left no legend of struggle or victory in the Marabar.
>
> (PI, 124)

So Hinduism and even Buddhism do not offer a key to the understanding of these caves. Thus we have to go back to aboriginal India for an answer to the problem posed by the Marabar caves, for they are not Buddhist or Hindu — 'all the Marabar Caves are Jain'. (PI, 217)

The second point that emerges from the above-quoted passage is that the caves stand for a degree of self-abnegation that is more complete than that of Buddha. This negation is reflected in the very shape and structure of these caves; they are hollow and bubble-shaped or empty as an Easter egg:

> One of them is rumoured within the boulder that swings on the summit of the highest of the hills; a bubble-shaped cave that has neither ceiling nor floor, and mirrors its own darkness in every direction infinitely. If the boulder falls and smashes, the cave will smash too – empty as an Easter egg. The boulder because of its hollowness sways in the wind, and even moves when a crow perches upon it: hence its name and the name of its stupendous pedestal: the Kawa Dol.
>
> (PI, 125)

Cosmic allegories often describe the world as having been born from an egg.[17] Hindu cosmology also conceives of the cosmos in terms of an egg – Brahma's egg which typifies the great Circle or O, a symbol for the universe. However, one should note that the caves are not like an egg, but like an egg-shell, and therefore they cannot symbolise positive, material reality. Perhaps they imply that reality is essentially hollow or in other words nothingness is reality. Darkness, chaos, emptiness, night, and nothingness out of which all existence came, seem to be the essence of the Marabar caves.

These caves are distinguished by another feature – they have a specific voice or an echo which is as indeterminate and indescribable as the caves themselves:

> The echo in a Marabar cave is not like these, it is entirely devoid of distinction. Whatever is said, the same monotonous noise replies, and quivers up and down the walls until it is absorbed into the roof. 'Boum' is the sound as far as the human alphabet can express it, or 'bou-oum', or 'ou-boum', – utterly dull.
>
> (PI, 145)

The echo 'bou-oum' or 'ou-boum' has been connected with the sacred Hindu word AUM or OM (A and U amalgamate to O) which is related to the cosmic egg or Brahma's egg – it is a visual–cum–aural symbol of the egg. However, the application of Hindu symbolism to the understanding of the caves raises difficulties. The mystical vedantic word OM or AUM (meaning 'aye', 'amen') is understood as an expression and affirmation of the totality of creation; it is a sound symbol of the whole of consciousness-existence, and at the same time its willing affirmation.[18] This is obviously in direct contradiction to the whole structure and function of the caves where the emphasis is all the time on denial and rejection of reality rather than its affirmation or acceptance.

The rejectionist function of the echo is clearly indicated by its impact on the listeners, particularly Western listeners. The confusion that Adela experiences during her visit to the caves and all the resultant disaster underline the nature of the echo and the caves. Even Mrs Moore, the one alien who comes close to the spirit of India, is perturbed by the echo. In some indescribable way, it seems to 'undermine her hold on life' and it whispers its message: 'Pathos, piety, courage – they exist, but are identical, and so is filth. Everything exists, nothing has value.' (PI, 147) Mrs Moore is scared; she tries to seek refuge in her own religion, but Christianity fails: 'poor little talkative Christianity, and she knew that all its divine words from "Let there be Light" to "It is finished" only amounted to "boum".' (PI, 148) Not only Christianity, but Islam too cannot cope with the challenge of the echo as Fielding reflects: 'And the mosque missed it too. Like himself, those shallow arcades provided but a limited asylum. "There is no God but God" doesn't carry us far through the complexities of matter and spirit.' (PI, 269)

However, the echo is not necessarily evil though it may appear to be that way in the first instance. Simply, these caves symbolise a vision of negation that is beyond the comprehension of even Hinduism which is armed with all the negative doctrines of *maya*. As suggested earlier, these caves are related to Jainism and we must turn to this aboriginal philosophy in order to understand the true character of the Marabar caves.[19]

Jainism, a post-Vedic heterodoxy, has its origins in the pre-Aryan culture of India. It is an atheistic, rejectionist philosophy that postulates a sharp distinction between soul and matter. The universe, according to the Jains, is eternal and uncreated, and contains two types of entities — souls or life monads (*jiva*) and non-living matter (*ajiva*). However, the life monads are obscured through their association with matter in accordance with the law of *karma* that causes the incessant round of reincarnation. The aim of the Jain is eventually to seek the liberation of the soul or life monad which will ascend to the summit of the cosmos where it will exist motionless for eternity in an infinity of empty space. The caves thus project the profoundly pessimistic vision of Jainism; they stand for the emptiness or the Nothing to which the Jain aspires.

Thus in terms of their vision of India as a Dark Power, the parallel between Forster and Kipling becomes very striking. For Kipling too India is a metaphysical being that frustrates all efforts at coming to terms with it, which negates all our values and modes of perception. For instance, the dark and ancient shrine of the Cow's Mouth in *The Naulahka* is similar to Forster's caves; here Tarvin, the hero of Kipling's novel, faces the emptiness and negation which Kipling sees as the essence of India. Here Tarvin also hears 'a malignant chuckle', the sound that comes from the rushing of the waters from an ancient tank through the Cow's jaws which is like the echo of the Marabar caves. Tarvin's experience of nothingness and horror in this shrine is similar to Adela's or Mrs Moore's reaction to the caves.

Moreover, given her nature, India manifests herself in certain ways that appear to us as negative, cruel, and even vicious. Here again the parallel with Kipling is unmistakable. In Kipling's works we have a long, woeful list of some of the negative traits of India — heat, dust, disease, death, corruption, riots, famines, ghosts, graveyards, to name a few. Forster too presents us with a similar catalogue. The little town of Chandrapore has its share of all these things. However, it is in terms of the psychologically crushing ways that the spirit of India adopts to destroy all relationships between Indians and non-Indians that one sees the extent to which Forster comes close to Kipling.

Kipling's view on the subject of the possibility of forming human relationships between the Indians and the British comes out sharply in the tragic love affairs between dusky-eyed Indian girls and god-like Englishmen. The most moving of these relationships is described in Kipling's story 'Without Benefit of Clergy' where the tender bond of love between Ameera and Holden is snapped suddenly through the silent, malignant power of India that visits them in the form of cholera and takes away both Ameera and his son from Holden's arms. Forster perhaps goes a step further than Kipling. As regards a romantic relationship between an Indian and a European, the possibility is not even considered by Forster. The moment Adela and Dr Aziz are alone in the primordial caves, Adela's suppressed sexuality comes to the fore and she has fantasies of being molested – this has nothing to do with love, romantic love, which at least is allowed in Kipling's stories. Forster's vision of India is bleaker than Kipling's; Forster's India negates the very possibility of love – all it can admit of is the possibility of rape as far as the two races are concerned.

THE INDIANS: HINDUS VERSUS MUSLIMS

Frustrated in his attempt at coming to grips with the metaphysical reality represented by India, Forster turns his attention to Indians in his search for some clue to the enigma of India. Here he is on slightly surer ground, though understanding the peoples of India is an equally baffling task. Just as there are a hundred Indias, there is no single, representative Indian: 'nothing embraces the whole of India' (PI, 143) and 'there is no such person in existence as the general Indian' (PI, 260), Forster admits. The Indians have their myriads of divisions and contradictions; the major divisions being along religious lines, especially between Hinduism and Islam.

Forster examines the gulf that separates Muslims and Hindus in some detail. The contrast between them is suggested in the very titles of his first and third sections – 'Mosque' and 'Temple' – which have obvious symbolic significance in the novel. The mosque seems to stand for openness, dialogue, brotherhood, social intercourse, and the possibility of establishing personal relationships between God and man and man and man. It is significant that it is in the mosque that Dr Aziz and Mrs Moore cross the racial barriers and come to a 'secret understanding of the heart' (PI, 21). The entire first section is concerned with the budding friendship between Aziz, Fielding, Mrs Moore, and Adela Quested despite all the hurdles in their way.

In a perceptive essay, 'The Mosque' (1920), Forster analyses the essential character of a mosque by differentiating it from a temple; the mosque, unlike a temple, does not arouse any definite sentiments:

It does not fulfil what is to most of us the function of a religious building: the outward expression of an inward ecstasy. It embodies no crises, leads up through no gradation of nave and choir, and employs no hierarchy of priests. Equality before God — so doubtfully proclaimed by Christianity — lies at the very root of Islam; and the mosque is essentially a courtyard for the Faithful to worship in, either in solitude or under due supervision.[20]

Forster particularly emphasises the human and social aspect of the mosque; it is pervaded by 'an atmosphere which, though supernatural, was not divine; men had produced it' (AH, 295).

The temple, in its very architecture, is an antithesis of the mosque. Instead of openness, fellowship, and social intercourse, the temple emphasises secrecy, solitude, and quiet contemplation. The structure of a Hindu temple, as Forster learned, symbolises the World Mountain in whose cavity one enters into a solitary meditation hoping for final mergence in the impersonally conceived *Brahman*. The interest in contemplative techniques and in concentration upon the inner self blends with the Hindu tendency to equate the macrocosm with the microcosm; hence the importance of the individual with little need of human fellowship. The essential aim of the entire Hindu ritual may be identified with knowledge of the self — this aim is expressed in the famous Vedic formula *tat tvam asi* ('That thou art') or in brief *atman* (self) is *Brahman* (the divine power pervading and sustaining the cosmos). This is fine philosophy, but it is rather discouraging as far as the development of a relationship between man and man is concerned.

The Muslims are represented by Dr Aziz, the central figure of the novel, and the circle of his friends — Hamidullah, Mahmood Ali, and the Nawab Bahadur. With the exception of the latter, they all belong to the middle-class, educated intelligentsia. Similarly, the Hindus that we meet in the novel are mostly middle-class professionals – Dr Panna Lal, Mr Das, and Professor Godbole.

What one immediately notices about Muslims is that like the British, they too are aliens in this land to a certain extent – their roots lie outside India, in neighbouring Afghanistan, Turkistan, Persia, and Arabia. What makes them less of an alien group than the British is that apart from their longer association with this land, their culture, despite its enormous differences from Indian culture, recognises the place of emotion and is thus more suited to India than Western culture.

The note of Muslim alienation in India is prominent in the novel. For instance, whenever Aziz and his friends sit down for an after-dinner conversation, they invariably go back to their glorious past or recite poetry written in the tradition of Persian *ghazal* (a highly conventional form of lyric poetry abounding in conceits) on the rather sad themes of the decay of Islam and transience of beauty. Among the modern poets, their favourite is Iqbal.[21] And when it comes to history, their favourite period is the Moghul period – Dr Aziz's heroes are Babur and Aurangzeb, especially Aurangzeb who struggled hard to put an Islamic stamp on India and is thus hated by Hindu historians. The one Moghul emperor whom the Hindus admire, namely Akbar, is rather disliked by Aziz for he tried to reconcile Islam with Hinduism through a new religion called *Din-i-Illahi*:

> 'But wasn't Akbar's new religion very fine? It was to embrace the whole of India?'
> 'Miss Quested, fine but foolish. You keep your religion, I mine. That is the best. Nothing embraces the whole of India, nothing, nothing, and that was Akbar's mistake.'

> (PI, 143)

The alienation of Muslims in India is further underlined by their relative ignorance of both India and Hinduism. For example, one of the great ironies of the novel is that Dr Aziz, who arranges the picnic to the Marabar caves, does not know anything about them:

His ignorance became evident, and was really rather a drawback.

In spite of his gay, confident talk, he had no notion how to treat this particular aspect of India; he was lost in it.

(PI, 140)

Similarly, later in the novel when Aziz is even working in a Hindu state, he does not understand the intricacies of the *Janam Ashtami* festival; he and his children go away from the Hindu crowd —they feel like foreigners in this land:

> Aziz did not pay attention to these sanctities, for they had no connection with his own; he felt bored, slightly cynical like his own dear Emperor Babur, who came down from the north and found in Hindustan no good fruit, no fresh water or witty conversation, not even a friend.

(PI, 301)

Given the great gulf between Islam and Hinduism, it is small wonder that there is not much social contact between the adherents of the two faiths. Hindus and Muslims see each other with fear, suspicion, and hostility; the spectre of communal riots haunts them constantly. Even when circumstances bring them together, the understanding does not last very long. After Aziz's acquittal, there is a temporary spirit of entente between the two communities, but even while they embrace each other, they are conscious of their deep-rooted animosities.

It may be noted that it is because of a similarity of position between Muslims and the British in India that Forster (and many other English writers on India including Kipling) shows an approving attitude towards Muslims. The Hindu baffles both Muslims and the British. The Hindu Professor Godbole is a case in point. Godbole represents a view of life which, profound though it may be, is so abstract that it is beyond the ken of Fielding, and by implication Forster himself. As Fielding prods him to express his opinion on the assault with which Aziz is charged, Godbole answers in what amounts to a riddle:

> 'When evil occurs, it expresses the whole of the universe. Similarly when good occurs.
>
> 'And similarly when suffering occurs, and so on and so forth, and everything is anything and nothing something. . . . Good and evil are different as their names imply. . . . they are both of them aspects of my Lord. He is present in the one, absent in the other, and

the difference between presence and absence is great. . . . Yet
absence implies presence, absence is not non-existence, and we are
therefore entitled to repeat, "Come, come, come, come".'

(PI, 175)

This sense of inscrutability and riddle of India is the keynote of the
festival of *Janam Ashtami* celebrated later in the novel, a section
heavily drawn from Forster's own experiences in Dewas. Here the
crowd led by Professor Godbole and the Rajah sings to the saint
Tukaram rather than to Lord Krishna whose birth they are celebrating and everything they do seems to be illogical and irrational:

They sang not even to the God who confronted them, but to a
saint; they did not one thing which the non-Hindu would feel
dramatically correct; this approaching triumph of India was a
muddle (as we call it), a frustration of reason and form.

(PI, 280)

I am not suggesting here that Forster is not alive to the message of love
and harmony that the birth of Krishna signifies; all I am trying to
point out is that the form in which this all-embracing vision is put is
not readily grasped by the non-Hindu mind accustomed to differen-
tiation and reason. This aspect of the festival is particularly emphasised in the account of it in *The Hill of Devi* where after eight days
of revelry, a disillusioned Forster comes to this conclusion: 'There is
no dignity, no taste, no form, and though I am dressed as a Hindu, I
shall never become one.' (HD, 107)

THE PRINCELY ORDER

In his exploration of India, the fundamental question that Forster
poses is: 'what is India?' or 'who understands India?' or perhaps 'who
embodies the spirit of India?' In the section on the Marabar caves, he
comes close to experiencing this mysterious being called India, but
that does not mean that he understands her. As far as understanding
her is concerned, he does not think that even Hinduism or Buddhism,
let alone Islam or Christianity, have fully come to terms with India.
However, he does concede that of all the existing modes of thought,
Hinduism has succeeded in scratching a few of the Marabar caves and
by implication the reality of India itself, though of course the key to

its understanding must be found in pre-Aryan, Dravidian ideologies such as Jainism. Nevertheless, Jainism itself, in its present form, is so mixed up with Hinduism that one has difficulties in isolating its pure, archaic elements.[22] Hence, perhaps one can never completely understand India as we have lost the instruments of proper exploration — all that we can hope for is to tend towards some partial understanding of this metaphysical reality, either through philosophies such as Jainism or through those Indians who appear to embody the spirit of India. And of all the Indians, it is the Hindu princes who, in Forster's view, seem to represent this spirit. The last chapter of *A Passage to India* and, in particular, *The Hill of Devi* project this point of view.

The Hill of Devi (1953) is a collection of letters that Forster wrote to his mother and other relatives during his visit to the State of Dewas Senior in 1912–13 and later in 1921 when he served there as private secretary to the Rajah, Sir Tukoji Rao, otherwise called Bapu Sahib. It is however not a haphazard collection of letters — it is a carefully edited work designed for a certain purpose. The purpose is defined in the preface where Forster significantly remarks that the letters are printed in the hope that 'the reader may share my bewilderment and pleasure at plunging into *an unknown world and meeting an unknown and possibly unknowable character*' (HD, 9. Italics mine). It is important to note the parallel Forster draws between the unknown world into which he was plunging (Dewas in particular and India in general) and the Rajah who was a perfect embodiment, a microcosm of this unknowable world. The other point that emerges here is that despite their inscrutability, both India and the Rajah are irresistible; the Rajah, we are told, 'was charming, he was loveable, *it was impossible to resist him or India*' (HD, 27. Italics mine). Again, it is significant that Forster connects the Rajah with the spirit of India.

Bapu Sahib is presented as a strange mixture of saint, genius and child who only responded to emotion and affection. He 'believed in the heart' (HD, 116) and Forster recalls how when he was depressed on his return to England, the Rajah sent him a message: 'Tell him from me to follow his heart and his mind will see everything clear.' (HD, 116)

This dependence on emotion rather than reason makes the Rajah unpredictable and full of contradictions — another parallel between him and the spirit of India. For instance, he can boast of his relationship with concubines and at the same time be deeply mystical and otherworldly or lapse into a prayer in the midst of a social get-together. No one can tell the Rajah's itinerary: 'I really don't know what happens next – one so seldom does' (HD, 28), Forster admits in frustration. Later, Forster extends his remark to the whole sub-continent: 'Little is clear cut in India' (HD, 39), and hence 'it is more difficult here than in England to get at the rights of a matter. Everything that happens is said to be one thing and proves to be another, and as it is further said in an unknown tongue I live in an haze.' (HD, 64)

The Rajah, a descendant of a very ancient line of Maratha nobility, believes in absolute personal rule though his kingdom or power does not extend very far. Education is deliberately kept to a minimum, public facilities are non-existent, and there is no real administrative machinery – the whole state, like India itself, is a big muddle. Some notion of this muddle may be formed by looking at the confusing geo-political status of the state of Dewas. It is in fact twin states – Dewas Senior and Dewas Junior, ruled by the descendants of two brothers who at some point in the past had the state partitioned. However, the division was made not by towns or sections, but by fields and streets. Moreover, one district is administered jointly. And there is one school to which each state appoints its own headmaster. Forster thus agrees with Malcolm Darling (Bapu Sahib's tutor who introduced Forster to the Rajah) in describing the state of Dewas as 'the oddest corner of the world outside Alice in Wonderland' (HD, 37).

The Rajah is in his element during the great Hindu festival of *Gokul Ashtami* or *Janam Ashtami* – the feast of the birth of Lord Krishna. This festival is as incomprehensible to the non-Hindu as the Rajah or India itself and this points to another link among them. There is however a certain Dionysiac aspect to this festival that can be appreciated even by a non-believer; one can relate the revelry, mirth, and dancing to something more ancient than Hinduism – it can all be seen as a vegetation cult celebrating the death and rebirth of fertility. Forster also realises that the festival has a definite mystical or spiritual message in that it symbolises the all-embracing quality of divine love. And yet, the form in which this message is cast makes it either incomprehensible or simply ludicrous.

The festival lasts eight days during which normal life comes to a standstill in Dewas. The entire population gathers around the shrine of Krishna where everything including the image of Krishna is 'smothered in mess and appallingness' (HD, 101). Forster goes on to comment:

What troubles me is that every detail, almost without exception, is fatuous and in bad taste. The altar is a mess of little objects, stifled with rose leaves, the walls are hung with deplorable oleographs, the chandeliers, draperies — everything is bad.

(HD, 106)

The atmosphere is simply stifling: there is deafening music from various bands (including one European one affecting a merry polka), children play games all over, officials yell at each other, and incense fumes suffocate the audience. The time of the birth of Krishna finally comes at midnight after a week of misery and waiting, and a tired Forster questions: 'Why, since he [Krishna] had been listening to hymns for eight days, he was now to be born was a puzzle to me.' (HD, 108)

Anyway the dancing Rajah announces the birth of the Lord Krishna which is followed by more noise — the horn brays, the cymbals clash, the drums beat, and elephants bellow. Everybody throws trays full of red powder in the air so that the whole aisle is filled with crimson smoke. And then begins the most ludicrous act — ceremonial games are played before the altar which consist of splashing butter onto each other's face or hitting the air with painted sticks. The image of Krishna is then taken out of the shrine in a procession led by the Rajah. All along the route the processionists are smeared with red and black powder by the people. And finally the procession crawls to the riverside where the ceremony of the drowning of the Town of Gokul is performed.

The festival of *Gokul Ashtami* reminds Forster of the feast of Adonis where the god is born, dies, and is carried to the water, all in a short time. Despite this awareness of the similarity of the Hindu ritual and the Greek one, Forster finds it too much to take. In order to retain his sanity, Forster leaves for Agra where, as he visits the Taj Mahal, he hears a *muezzin* calling the faithful to prayers; he feels that he is back on solid ground after the bedlam of *Gokul Ashtami*:

'There is no God but God.' I do like Islam, though I have had to come through Hinduism to discover it. After all the mess and profusion and confusion of Gokul Ashtami, where nothing ever stopped or need ever have begun, it was like standing on a mountain.

(HD, 127)

Similarly, on his way back to England, he felt 'relief' on passing from the Hindu Dewas to the Muslim Deccan where he stopped to see his close friend Syed Ross Masood; the relief was again based on coming to a world which he could understand: 'I have come too into a world whose troubles and problems are intelligible to me: Dewas made much ado about nothing and no ado where a little would have been seemly.' (HD, 154)

Despite all these expressions of relief that he felt on getting out of Dewas, one must note that he loved the Rajah — 'I hated leaving him', Forster confesses (HD, 154). His deep affection for Bapu Sahib and perhaps the whole of the fast-fading princely order of India is unmistakable. In showing this affection, Forster is fully aware that he may be accused of having feudalistic or reactionary sympathies, but that does not matter for he feels a genuine admiration for the India represented by her quaint *rajahs* and *nawabs*. In his own words, *The Hill of Devi* is a record of 'a vanished civilization' and while he knows that 'some will rejoice it has vanished', he also knows that 'others will feel that something precious has been thrown away amongst the rubbish — something which might have been saved' (HD, 10). Forster makes it quite clear to which side he belongs.

At this point some information about Indian princes is in order. On the eve of independence, there were about five hundred *rajahs, maharajahs, nawabs*, and *jagirdars* who ruled one third of India and a quarter of her population. The Indian princes were allowed to retain their thrones as long as they remained loyal to the King-Emperor (represented by the Viceroy in New Delhi) and ceded to him the control of their foreign affairs and defence. Most of these princes were a strange breed who gave rise to a number of myths about their fabulous wealth, teeming harems, marble palaces, tiger hunts, elephants, jewels, and extravagant self-indulgence. Generally speaking, they showed little interest in improving the lot of their subjects and tended to be petty despots. The British let the princes get away with almost anything as long as they remained loyal to them, though in theory they could be dismissed for misrule. The inevitable result was a series of grateful reactionary princes who stood like a rock against the nationalist movements that swept the rest of India.[23]

Forster's 1922 essay, 'The Mind of the Indian Native State', clearly shows that he was fully aware of the reactionary nature of the Indian princes. He knew that the Indian Government was giving increasing consideration to the princes because of their usefulness as 'counter-weights against the new Nationalism' (AH, 353). He had first-hand knowledge of the tyrannical and autocratic ways of these princes who lived in a dream world of their own with no sympathy or understanding of the aspirations of their subjects: 'It is neither in their tradition nor to their interest,' Forster observes, 'that India should become a nation.' (AH, 353) Later in the essay, Forster makes a perceptive analysis of the contrast between native states and British India which proves his political acumen:

> History is full of ironies, and it is strange to reflect that those parts of India which the British deprived of independence are now the most independent. Not only is the individual safer and freer in them, but he has, if he chooses to take it, a greater share of political power. He may hate the British and have good reasons for doing so, but he would not exchange their yoke for an Indian Prince's; so that the Native States can only be enlarged or re-created if the principle of self-determination is ignored.
>
> (AH, 362)

And he goes on to declare:

> An alliance between the British and the Princes against the rest of India could only lead to universal disaster, yet there are people on both sides who are foolish enough to want it.
>
> (AH, 363)

In spite of such a clear understanding of the issue, *The Hill of Devi* is an apology for the princely order of India. The only way in which one can explain this apparent contradiction is that while Forster's head leads him one way, his heart remains with the quaint *rajahs* and the life they represent.

THE RAJ IN ACTION

Apart from being a philosophic inquiry into the nature of reality and the human condition, *A Passage to India* has an obvious political level on which it can be read as an account of the Raj in India. The political theme, though secondary, is important to the understanding of the novel, as Forster himself pointed out that 'the political side of it was an aspect I wanted to express'.[24] Forster's treatment of this subject is far from superficial; here he raises some essential questions about the meaning and validity of the imperial idea and as to how imperialism affects inter-personal as well as inter-racial relationships.

The opening scene of the novel introduces the political theme right away. The division between the British rulers and native subjects is brought home with great clarity by the physical separation of the low-lying, squalid, and haphazardly-built Indian section of Chandrapore from the clean and orderly civil station on the rise where the Europeans live. The character of the two communities is skilfully suggested in the topography and structure of their respective residential areas which have nothing in common – the civil station 'shares nothing with the city except the overarching sky' (PI, 10). As opposed to the Indian section, the civil station is 'sensibly planned' with 'a red-brick club on its brow' and bungalows disposed along 'roads that intersect at right angles' – these roads, named after victorious British generals, are 'symbolic of the net Great Britain had thrown over India' (PI, 18).

The hide-bound nature of the 'Anglo-Indian'[25] society is studied in considerable detail. The 'Anglo-Indian' officials regard themselves as living symbols of the Raj and behave as an army of occupation; they dislike and distrust Indians and do not want to have anything to do with them except for a master-servant relationship. The *memsahib*'s attitude towards the Indians is even harder than that of many *pukka sahibs*; her strongest link with India is through her hordes of servants in a strictly feudal relationship.[26] It is thus quite natural for Mrs Callendar to remark that 'the kindest thing one can do to a native is to let him die' (PI, 28). In response to Mrs Moore's ironical query, 'How if he went to heaven?' she replies with perfect candour: 'He can go where he likes as long as he doesn't come near me. They give me the creeps.' (PI, 28)

There is no question of a social intercourse between the two communities, and thus Adela's and Mrs Moore's desire to get to know real India and Indians appals the entire 'Anglo-Indian' community of Chandrapore. Ronny frankly tells his mother and Adela: 'we don't come across them socially' (PI, 28). Nevertheless, a half-hearted attempt is made at a social meeting with some Indians in order to satisfy the two newly-arrived English ladies, but the Bridge Party fails to bridge any gap between the two sides. The Indians and the English stand massed at different corners of the lawn; the party is doomed because of the haughty attitude of the British typified by the hostess, Mrs Burton, who instructs Mrs Moore to remember: 'You're superior to them, anyway. Don't forget that. You're superior to everyone in India except one or two of the Ranis, and they're on an equality.' (PI, 42)

The hub of social life for the 'Anglo-Indians' is their red-brick club – an almost 'holy' institution where they learn the norms of behaviour in the caste-ridden society of India. The club, which was normally private, was one of the most interesting institutions developed by the Raj; it was, in the words of George Orwell, 'the spiritual citadel, the real seat of the British power, the Nirvana for which native officials and millionaires pine in vain'.[27] The club, out of bounds for the natives,[28] was a social centre for both men and women though women had no official standing. All the senior officials belonged to it and it was almost a ritual to go to the club. If you did not belong to the club, you were an outcast or a rebel. The membership was dependent entirely upon occupation, and discrimination over status was often preserved. The club at Chandrapore is a typical 'Anglo-Indian' club which is held up to ridicule by Forster. Here one sees the little tin gods of Chandrapore in their human frailty interested in shouting '*Koi-Hai*' (which was the call for the servants to come and attend), drinking their *chotapegs* or *burrapegs* of Scotch, or indulging in small talk about *shikar* and scandal.

In many ways the 'Anglo-Indian' world is monotonous – even its meals are that way:

> Julienne soup full of bullety bottled peas, pseudo-cottage bread, fish full of branching bones, pretending to be plaice, more bottled peas with the cutlets, trifle, sardines on toast: the menu of Anglo-India. A dish might be added or subtracted as one rose or fell in the official scale . . . but the tradition remained; the food of exiles, cooked by servants who did not understand it.
>
> (PI, 47)

Their life is untouched by literature or art. 'Their ignorance of the Arts', Forster comments, 'was notable . . . the Arts were bad form.' (PI, 40)

The 'Anglo-Indian' official also conforms to type. The public school spirit dominates him – he is efficient, authoritarian, well-disciplined, and a firm believer in the Empire. It is all work from his point of view – 'we're out here to do justice and keep the peace. Them's my sentiments. India isn't a drawing-room' (PI, 49), Ronny tells his mother frankly. In holding such a view of their role in India, the 'Anglo-Indian' officials perhaps pose as arrogant gods, but in

Ronny's opinion that does not really hurt anyone for they are 'doing good in this country' (PI, 49). And he goes on to elaborate:

> I am out here to work, mind, to hold this wretched country by force. I'm not a missionary or a Labour Member or a vague sentimental sympathetic literary man. I'm just a servant of the Government; it's the profession you wanted me to choose myself, and that's that. We're not pleasant in India, and we don't intend to be pleasant. We've something more important to do.
>
> (PI, 50)

Ronny's belief in the doctrine of action brings him pretty close to some of Kipling's ideal civil servants, and he does prove himself later in the novel. Around Mohurram time, Chandrapore is engulfed in communal tension and a familiar riot situation builds up. The Muslims make *tazias* (paper towers) too high to pass under the branches of a certain *pepul* tree sacred to the Hindus. Someone cuts down the branches of the tree and a clash between the two communities is imminent. Turton and Ronny get to work immediately. They form conciliation committees, chart a route for the procession acceptable to the parties, and thus prevent the situation from taking an uglier turn. It is this kind of work which seems to be a justification for the Raj:

> But Ronny had not disliked his day, for it proved that the British were necessary in India; there would certainly have been bloodshed without them. His voice grew complacent again; he was here not to be pleasant but to keep the peace.
>
> (PI, 93)

Forster however makes us see the other side of the coin, the ugly side of the Raj, as well. The British can be efficient, fair, and impartial administrators as long as they are solving a problem involving Indians alone, but they lose their cool as soon as the clash is between themselves and the Indians. This can be seen in the way the naked machinery of the Raj comes into action during the trial of Dr Aziz for the alleged assault on Adela. Adela, who was never popular with the 'Anglo-Indian' community, suddenly becomes their darling for now she is a symbol of English womanhood violated by an Indian. The scene at the club after the arrest of Aziz is hysterical; it has the air of the Residency at Lucknow at the time of the Mutiny. They are all reminded that they are an outpost of the Empire, and that they must teach a lesson to the natives. This incident thus arouses deep-seated racial emotions in an otherwise dull and emotionless community:

> All over Chandrapore that day the Europeans were putting aside their normal personalities and sinking themselves in their community. Pity, wrath, heroism, filled them, but the power of putting two and two together was annihilated.
>
> (PI, 162)

Mr McBryde, the District Superintendent of Police, has his own theory about climatic zones which he does not hesitate to expound:

> All unfortunate natives are criminals at heart, for the simple reason that they live south of latitude 30. They are not to blame, they have not a dog's chance — we should be like them if we settled here.
>
> (PI, 164)

He even tries to convince Fielding into accepting his point of view:

> But, you see, Fielding, as I've said to you once before, you're a schoolmaster, and consequently you come across these people at their best. That's what puts you wrong. They can be charming as boys. But I know them as they really are, after they have developed into men.
>
> (PI, 166)

In a way the 'Anglo-Indians' are delighted that things went wrong for Adela as this seems to prove them right. The collector now openly asserts the 'Anglo-Indian' position on the subject of contact with Indians:

> I have never known anything but disaster result when English people and Indians attempt to be intimate socially. Intercourse, yes. Courtesy by all means. Intimacy — never, never. The whole weight of my authority is against it.
>
> (PI, 161)

The case of Dr Aziz is set before the Hindu magistrate Das, Ronny's assistant, as the lawyers for Aziz have objected to Ronny on personal grounds. The civil station finds it hard to accept the idea of an

Indian magistrate trying the case involving an English girl. Ronny longs for the old days when an Englishwoman would not have had to appear in the court at all. In the end he calms down thinking that Das dares not incur his disfavour and that 'conviction was inevitable; so better let an Indian pronounce it' (PI, 210).

The 'Anglo-Indian' complacency about the result of the trial soon runs into snags. Fielding openly sides with Aziz and Mrs Moore, the other English person present at the picnic, refuses to be dragged into the affair; she is in fact quite convinced of Aziz's innocence. Adela too is not that sure: 'Ronny,' she tells him at one point, 'he's innocent; I made an awful mistake.' (PI, 198) As Mrs Moore could be a bad influence on Adela, Ronny packs her off to England though she never reaches there; she dies at sea on her way home.

The trial of Dr Aziz arouses an equally strong emotional reaction on the Indian side — they too see it in racial terms as the repression of a fellow Indian (even though he is a Muslim) by the British. Thus for the time being both Hindus and Muslims, despite their own tensions and differences, rally together. The sweepers of the district go on strike, a number of Muslim ladies observe fast in protest, and students stage a demonstration. The Nawab Bahadur renounces the title awarded to him by the Indian Government and finances the defence of Aziz. Aziz's friends (who are lawyers themselves) engage Amritrao, a Hindu barrister from Calcutta who is notoriously anti-British, so that the case may be given a wider political colouring.

The defence asks for Mrs Moore's evidence, and when the Magistrate disallows the request, he is accused of collusion with the British. Pleader Hamidullah leaves the court in a rage, and the Indians pick up the name Mrs Moore (Indianised into Esmiss Esmoor) whom they invoke like a goddess. The chanting of the name of Mrs Moore seems to have a deep psychological impact on Adela; she begins to see things clearly; and in the midst of her testimony she, to the horror of her community, recants and withdraws all charges against Dr Aziz. In doing so, she displays great integrity and courage for this means not only the renunciation of her people but giving up her marriage with Ronny. However, Aziz and other Indians fail to appreciate this courageous act; they, like the 'Anglo-Indians', want total revenge.

The one person who keeps his balance throughout the story is Fielding, the principal of the local college. A spokesman for Forster in many ways, Fielding is a humanist, an agnostic liberal, a rationalist, and a believer in personal relationships.[29] From the very beginning he is shown to be different from the rest of the 'Anglo-Indians' in

Chandrapore; he does not really socialise with them that much; and it is he who seeks the friendship of Indians, particularly Dr Aziz. He believes that the world is 'a globe of men who are trying to reach one another and can best do so by the help of good will plus culture and intelligence – a creed ill-suited to Chandrapore' (PI, 62). Naturally he is seen by other 'Anglo-Indians' as 'a disruptive force' whose 'ideas are fatal to caste' (PI, 62).

Aziz and Fielding do become friends. Aziz, in an act symbolic of trust and intimacy, shows Fielding the photograph of his dead wife. Fielding appreciates this gesture though he does not share his past completely with Aziz. There are obvious differences in their precepts, attitudes, and values which create difficulties in the development of their friendship. This difference may for example be gathered from Fielding's criticism, 'You are so fantastic. . . . Your emotions never seem in proportion to their objects' (PI, 246) which is countered by an angry Aziz: 'Is emotion a sack of potatoes, so much the pound, to be measured out? Am I a machine?' (PI, 247)

The greatest strain on their friendship is the strain of imperialism. Occasionally, Fielding's conversation with the Indians turns to politics and it is here that he feels most uncomfortable. 'How is England justified in holding India?' (PI, 108) Hamidullah asks him. And a non-plussed Fielding replies: 'I'm out here personally because I needed a job. I cannot tell you why England is here or whether she ought to be here. It's beyond me.' (PI, 108) The Indian lawyer goes on to argue: 'Is it fair an Englishman should occupy one when Indians are available?' and Fielding does not know what to say:

> There is only one answer to a conversation of this type: 'England holds India for her good.' Yet Fielding was disinclined to give it. . . . He said, 'I'm delighted to be here too – that's my answer, there's my only excuse. I can't tell you anything about fairness. . . . Still, I'm glad it's happened, and I'm glad I'm out here. However big a badmash [ruffian] one is – if one's happy in consequence, that is some justification.'
>
> (PI, 108)

This is no reasoning at all and naturally it bewilders his Indian friends. Fielding, and by implication Forster himself, rejects the traditional justification of imperialism that the natives are incapable of ruling themselves; he sees imperialism as immoral, and yet he is not willing to quit India. Both Fielding and Forster seem to think that the

political tensions in India are mainly because of lack of personal
relationship between the two races, and that understanding, good
will, and kindness could solve the problem though perhaps they also
know that the time for such a solution is past:

> The decent Anglo-Indian of today realizes that the great blunder of
> the past is neither political nor economic nor educational, but
> social. . . . The mischief has been done, and though friendship
> between individuals will continue and courtesies between high
> officials increase, there is little hope now of spontaneous in-
> tercourse between two races. . . . Never in history did ill-breeding
> contribute so much towards the dissolution of an Empire.[30]

The trial of Dr Aziz, a direct outcome of the realities of
imperialism, puts this friendship between Aziz and Fielding to
maximum pressure and eventually forces each of them to retreat into
his own community. Aziz recognises his identity as an Indian or
rather an Indian Muslim and turns anti-British; the possibility of
Indo-British friendship no longer excites him. The British Raj is a
constant assault on his dignity and he longs to shake the dust of
Anglo-India off his feet. He finally quits British India and takes up
service in the Hindu state of Mau through the help of Professor
Godbole, who is now the state's Minister of Education. Aziz chooses a
Hindu state instead of a Muslim one because his anti-British feeling
has turned him into a nationalist. He now speaks of Indian unity, and
standing motionless in Mau in the rain, he thinks that he is an Indian at
last.

Fielding too changes somewhat. He goes back to England, marries
Mrs Moore's daughter Stella, and returns to India to take up a
position in the Education Department of the Government of India.
He is now part of the establishment and his liberalism is watered
down a bit. This is apparent when he comes to Mau on an inspection
of the local school and meets Aziz for the last time. The former
warmth is missing on both sides; Aziz tells him curtly: 'I wish no
Englishman or Englishwoman to be my friend.' (PI, 298) Fielding
too has hardened; he retorts with a sneer: 'Away from us, Indians go
to seed at once. Look at the King Emperor High School! Look at you,
forgetting your medicine and going back to charms.' (PI, 316) Aziz
gets excited and shouts back: 'Clear out, all you Turtons and Burtons.
We wanted to know you ten years back — now it's too late.' 'Who do
you want instead of the English? The Japanese?' jeers Fielding. Aziz

shouts again, 'India shall be a nation! No foreigners of any sort!' and
dancing with rage he yells:

> Clear out you fellows, double quick, I say. We may hate one
> another, but we hate you most. If I don't make you go, Ahmed
> will, Karim will, if it's fifty five-hundred years we shall get rid of
> you, yes, we shall drive every blasted Englishman into the sea, and
> then . . . you and I shall be friends.
>
> (PI, 317)

However, in the atmosphere of love generated by *Janam Ashtami*
and the mystical presence of the spirit of Mrs Moore (who revisits
them in the tangible shape of her son and daughter), the friendship of
Aziz and Fielding is healed to a certain extent. Aziz and Fielding go
out for their last ride together in the Mau jungles and the
reconciliation is a success somehow:

> All the stupid misunderstandings had been cleared up, but socially
> they had no meeting-place. He had thrown in his lot with Anglo-
> India by marrying a countrywoman, and he was acquiring some of
> its limitations, and already felt surprise at his own past heroism.
> Would he to-day defy all his own people for the sake of a stray
> Indian? Aziz was a memento, a trophy, they were proud of each
> other, yet they must inevitably part.
>
> (PI, 314)

Yet this is a far cry from an attainment of inter-racial harmony – that
possibility is completely killed by the taint of imperialism – time and
place forbid a full-scale friendship on individual or national level:

> 'Why can't we be friends now?' said the other, holding him
> affectionately. 'It's what I want. It's what you want.'
>   But the horses didn't want it – they swerved apart; the earth
> didn't want it, sending up rocks through which riders must pass
> single file; the temples, the tank, the jail, the palace, the birds, the
> carrion, the Guest House, that came into view as they issued from
> the gap and saw Mau beneath: they didn't want it, they said in their
> hundred voices, 'No, not yet,' and the sky said, 'No, not there.'
>
> (PI, 317)

CONCLUSION: APPROACHES TO REALITY

A Passage to India is thick with symbols, images, and thematic patterns which defy simplistic interpretation. At the deepest level, Forster is here concerned with building a passage to India in a philosophic sense; he is concerned with understanding the metaphysical entity called India. His vision of India, as symbolised by the Marabar caves, comes close to that of Kipling: it is essentially a journey into an area of darkness, the realm of *nada*, and hence, as he himself acknowledges, incomprehensible.[31] It is thus small wonder that empirical explorations are unreliable. What finally emerges in the novel is an indeterminate, shapeless India with a hundred faces suggestive of a microcosm of reality or rather the complexity of reality.

In order to understand India, Forster turns to an investigation of various Indian communities, their beliefs and traditions, their divisions and contradictions, hoping to find a unifying pattern somewhere. This rather objective approach makes him see that despite enormous differences between Hindus and Muslims, their civilisations are better suited to reach the unknown and the mysterious for they recognise the place of emotion, which is missing in the Western civilisation. The mystical poetry of Ghalib or Iqbal and the festival of *Janam Ashtami* underline this point.

The Western civilisation is represented by the British who happen to rule India at the time. This brings Forster to another relevant subject – his favourite theme of human relationships – and he turns his attention to Indo–British relationships in the context of the Raj. At this level the political aspect becomes important to the meaning of the novel. Forster gives a credible and detailed portrayal of life in India at the time, and indicates the particular problems faced by all, especially the problem of communication between individuals and various ethnic groups.

The major hurdle in the development of inter-personal and inter-racial harmony is correctly diagnosed to stem as much from human limitations as from the atmosphere created by imperialism. Forster paints the 'Anglo-Indian' world with stark realism and debunks most of the myths lying behind the imperial idea, particularly the notion of racial or cultural superiority. He knows that the Raj rests on fear and he rejects the British use of force. He is equally scornful of the public school code exemplified by Ronny Heaslop and the racial theoretician McBryde, who believes that all natives born in the tropics are criminals at heart. McBryde was born in Karachi and seems to contradict his own theory for, after attacking Aziz's sexual morality, he is caught committing adultery with Miss Derek.

Forster's anti-imperial stance is further indicated by his sympathetic, sensitive, and highly authentic portrayal of Indian society and Indian characters. Dr Aziz, the central figure of *A Passage to India*, is perhaps the first fully developed Indian character in the English novel. And the Indian and English social scenes are also carefully juxtaposed to highlight the warm vitality of the former and the cold sterility of the latter.

However, it may also be observed that Dr Aziz, despite his charm and sensitivity, is in certain ways presented like a child – the stock image of an Indian character in Anglo-Indian fiction. Aziz is a creature of emotion and does not know how to adjust himself to the reality of a situation. Although he is a Western-trained doctor of medicine, his interest lies in sentimental poetry or religion; once away from the British influence, his skill as a medical man deteriorates fast – in the state of Mau for instance 'he had to drop inoculation and such Western whims . . . he let his instruments rust, ran his hospital at half steam' (PI, 288). Hence the implied need for a rational, paternal figure supplied by the British, such as Fielding.

Moreover, despite all his sympathy for the Indians and his rejection of the imperial idea, it is curious to note that Forster is not really interested in granting freedom to India. Instead he is at pains to point out the benefits of the British connection such as rule of law, introduction of modern education, and relief work in times of famine. As late as 1945, when he visited India for the last time, he refused to commit himself on the issue of Indian independence. In his essay 'India Again' (1946) he records his impressions of his trip, and in a Kipling-like manner, he dismisses the Indian preoccupation with politics: 'Their attitude is "first we must find the correct political solution, and then we deal with other matters"' (TC, 324). 'I think the attitude is unsound,' Forster remarks and he goes on to elaborate:

There is still poverty, and, since I am older today and more thoughtful, it is the poverty, the malnutrition, which persists like a ground-swell beneath the pleasant froth of my immediate experience. I do not know what political solution is correct. But I do know that people ought not to be so poor and to look so ill, and that rats ought not to run about them as I saw them doing in a labour camp at Bombay.

(TC, 324)

Towards the end of this essay, he repeats apologetically: 'To the tragic problem of India's political future I can contribute no solution.' (TC, 331)

3 E. J. Thompson

Edward John Thompson (1886–1946) is a relatively unknown figure of minor literary merit, though in any discussion of English writers working within the context of the Raj in its twilight days, he must be placed high on the list, for he wrote extensively on India. Moreover, in the thirties, like Kipling at the turn of the century,[1] he was considered an expert on India and his views had an influence on British public opinion. Both of his parents were Wesleyan missionaries who spent quite some time in South India though Edward was not born there.[2] After his graduation from London University he was ordained and was sent in 1910 to the Wesleyan College at Bankura, Bengal.

Thompson taught English literature at Bankura, wrote poetry, studied Bengali, and sought intellectual stimulation outside his academic duties, meeting Rabindranath Tagore in 1913 and eventually coming to understand Bengali poetry better than any other Englishman.[3] He became chaplain in 1916 to the 7th Division, went through the Mesopotamian and Palestinian campaigns, and was awarded the MC. He had married in 1919 and in 1920 had returned to Bankura as acting principal. This was a time of crisis in India, triggered by the massacre in 1919 of peaceful Indians by General Dyer at Jallianwala Bagh, Amritsar. Although hitherto not interested in politics, Thompson was deeply moved by this incident and opposed British approval of Dyer's action. From this moment onwards his writings take a political colouring. He began to understand the genuine basis of Indian bitterness against the British – this is illustrated by *The Other Side of the Medal* (1925), which gives the Indian point of view on the Mutiny. He now became convinced that Indians and British could not really be reconciled with each other without the granting of self-rule, if not total independence, to India.

He returned to England in 1923 to devote himself to full-time writing, resigning from the Wesleyan ministry. He was lecturer in Bengali at Oxford to Indian Civil Service probationers (1923–33) and later a research fellow in Indian History at Oriel College

(1936—46). By now he was in complete favour of a full-fledged Indian independence, and during all these years he worked hard to create a climate of opinion suitable for the final transfer of power in 1947. A friend of Gandhi, Tagore, Nehru, and other Indian, particularly Hindu, leaders, he also endeavoured to strengthen the cultural and spiritual ties which he hoped would always unite the two countries. He revisited India in 1932, 1937, and finally in late 1939.

Thompson was a versatile writer — he tried his hand at almost everything — poetry, fiction, drama, biography, history, expository prose. Although his fiction has only minor artistic worth, it remains valuable as a testimony of India's social and political history. Among his novels, *An Indian Day* (1927), *A Farewell to India* (1931), and *An End of the Hours* (1938) form a trilogy of which *A Farewell to India* is the best known. The historical and expository works of particular relevance to this study are *A History of India* (1927), *The Reconstruction of India* (1930), *A Letter from India* (1932), *Rise and Fulfilment of British Rule in India* (1934), and *Enlist India for Freedom!* (1940).

I will first examine Thompson's expository writings and then I will move on to a study of his fiction, concentrating on *A Farewell to India*.

HISTORICAL OBJECTIVITY: NON-FICTION

In his expository writings, Thompson displays a gradual development of historical objectivity, liberal humanism, and an application of the spirit of reconciliation. All of these attitudes are, for example, explicitly stated in the preface to *Rise and Fulfilment of British Rule in India* (written in collaboration with G. T. Garratt),[4] and the authors try to live up to their stated purposes. They point out the 'crude racial passions' and 'gross ingratitude' that the British displayed at the time of the Mutiny; the rise of extreme bureaucracy in the post-Mutiny period; the imposition of an oppressive land tenure system which put the *ryot* (peasantry) at the mercy of the *banias* (money-lenders); the inevitable rise of nationalism at the turn of the century; the barbarity of Dyer's Amritsar massacre of 1919; the half-hearted experiment with dyarchy and the Round Table Conferences of the early thirties. In the end, the writers place emphasis on solving the social and economic problems of India, and they conclude with a call for India's freedom:

The moral and social prestige lost to the West by the War can never be recovered, but there is no reason why a far healthier relationship should not develop, and the great sub-continent of India form part of a noble comity of nations within the British Commonwealth. It is in this belief that this book has been written. [5]

This categorical call for India's independence marks a shift from Thompson's earlier attitude in such works as *A History of India* (1927) and *The Reconstruction of India* (1930). *A History of India* places the emphasis on the British work in India, and here he appeals to Indians not to continue extravagant laudation of their past or their spiritual qualities in order to detract from the British reconstruction of India:

> In the end it will be acknowledged by all that it was fortunate that new life came to India. Some of the outward gifts of British power are so familiar that they pass unnoticed; men forget how amazing it is that there should be peace and security over so vast a country. But it is nonsense to say that India has gained only material things. . . . The very soul of India has been changed, and she has been made capable, as she was not before, of giving her own noble gifts, first of all to her own sons, whatever their creed or caste, and then to the world. [6]

Thompson's vacillation between sympathy for the Indian cause and the defence of his own people particularly marks *The Reconstruction of India*. The book was aimed at an American audience which he thought misinformed on the subject of Indian nationalism and the British Raj. After giving a brief historical account of British rule in India, he comes to the issue of nationalism, which had aroused American sympathy and support. Referring to the Indian demand for total independence, he states:

> There is the 'clear-cut course' the National Congress demands. Independence. The Congress has given us the option between finding an immediate complete solution – which it cannot find itself – and the inauguration of a period of bloodshed and administrative chaos (for this is what Independence would mean). . . . There is 'Dominion Status' – the right way out, but how beset with difficulty! Immediate, full Dominion Status would merely make a fool of India, or, rather, put her where she cannot help making a fool of herself (and an extremely unhappy fool). [7]

At this point he does not think that India is ready for dominion status for, and here he puts the blame on Britain, she has not been trained for the job; the legacy of post-Mutiny hatred led to the complete dissociation of Indians from the processes of government; there was a racial severance. In this context he speaks of his admiration for Forster who portrays this racial gulf so successfully:

> E. M. Forster's *A Passage to India*, a book I resented when it came out, but later, on re-reading, admired greatly (though with reservations, of no importance here), was hard on Indians and British alike. Yet the reluctant conclusion of an English official who hated the book was: 'But hang it all! It's an *exact* picture of provincial life, in an up-country station, before the War.' If it is not, then what are we to make of Kipling?
>
> (RI, 42–3)

At this stage, his views on the Congress are less admiring than what they develop into later on. He traces the evolution of the Congress from a moderate party to what he calls a violent one, noting its agitation against the 1905 partition of Bengal, its association with Muslims in the Khilafat Movement during the First World War, the launching of the non-cooperation movement, its adoption of a communal character and the consequent parting of the way from Muslims. He does not hesitate to criticise Gandhi: 'Mahatma Gandhi is not a great thinker', he declares (RI, 135); he notes Gandhi's 'infantile confusion of thought' (RI, 135); and ridicules Gandhi for his paeans to the cow. This, of course, is balanced by his praise for some of his qualities, particularly Gandhi's humanity and charisma.

Coming back to the question of self-government, he reiterates that dominion status is India's right, but as long as the terrible social evils (such as pointed out by Miss Mayo's *Mother India*) and communal clashes continue there can be little hope of its grant. Secondly, he feels that the Indian masses need 'good administration' and Indians have to prove their ability in this respect. He is convinced that 'if England walked out of India, India could not escape that bitterest of wars, a religious war' (RI, 240). So for Thompson the British presence is justified at the time; he looks forward to a ripe moment for the transfer of power; and in the meantime he wants his countrymen to take Indian thought and literature seriously and build understanding with Indians so that there should be no bitterness between them when

India becomes a free nation. Eventually he would like to see India as a full member of the Commonwealth:

> I have no more love for the Empire, as that word and things are by many understood, than I have for any other manifestation of the spirit of aggression. But to many of us the Empire is a preparation for the peace of all Nations, a commonwealth which will not absorb other peoples but will show the way for all to find the fullest freedom.
>
> (RI, 276–7)

After 1930, Thompson's views become more pro-India and pro-Congress. His later works establish this point conclusively. For example, in *A Letter from India* (1932), Thompson deals in detail with the episode of the Amritsar massacre which was catalytic in arousing his sympathy for Indians. He gives an objective account of the incident and justly remarks that Dyer's action did irreparable damage to the Raj and that he shot away more than he preserved.[8] *A Letter from India* gives a true picture of the complex situation in India upon Gandhi's arrest, after the collapse of the Irwin-Gandhi pact of 1931 when the fragile peace could explode at any moment. Thompson argues for the legitimacy of the nationalists' cause, expressing great admiration for Gandhi and his policy of non-violence:

> His 'non-violence' has not only given a unique quality to the Indian struggle (powerfully drawing out the sympathy of the outside world). It has set a reciprocal quality on the British 'repression' of that struggle. At our house he emphasized the honour that would be India's if she won freedom without recourse to violence. I replied that it would be an equal distinction for my own people.
>
> (LI, 39–40)

This admiration is, however, tinged with his fear of Gandhi's losing control over the party:

> It is perhaps true that Mr. Gandhi is still the main defence against a bloody outbreak. Certainly he has exercised a restraining influence on his followers. But the last few years have seen him growing eccentric, increasingly tolerant of lapses from the incredibly lofty ideals associated with his name. He is not the man he was.
>
> (LI, 41)

Fears of violence turn his attention to the North West Frontier Province where the Red Shirt Movement aiming at the ousting of the British through force was in full swing. The British were busy repressing the movement and the Kohat shootings, 'a second Amritsar', had just taken place. Thompson underlines the violent nature of this movement by quoting from the speeches of its leader, Abdul Ghaffar Khan, and he observes that the Red Shirt Movement must not be taken lightly.

Then he casts a brief look at the princely India, and finds them in favour of a 'federation' so long as they have safeguards for their internal sovereignty. They continue to indulge in extravagance while their people languish in abject poverty; they are in league with the reactionary elements among the British in order to preserve their autocracy. But he questions how long the princes or the British can keep things this way; he sees no justification for the preservation of the princely order. [9]

However, at the time of writing *A Letter from India*, he still believed that an abrupt departure of the British could cause a great deal of suffering:

Indians resent the argument that Britain has a 'trust' in India. I do not use it, and many other Englishmen have ceased to use it. Yet the only thing worth striving for is to lessen human suffering; and an abrupt departure of the British from India, which I wish to God were possible, would cause very great suffering, though we should be the gainers in everything but self-respect.

(LI, 30–1)

In his 1940 book *Enlist India for Freedom!* he takes up the theme of social and political conditions in India, and has now moved to the point where he feels that India is ready for freedom. He poses the question: 'Why can we not say to India, "Be one of us! And free?" '[10] He refers to the enormous progress Indians have made in all fields, and sees no reason why power cannot be transferred immediately:

I do not understand what constitutes fitness for a natural right. India's neighbours, Siam, Tibet, Nepal, Iran, are independent. I suppose this is because they are more fit for self-government. In these last years I have often wondered if the British are fit for self-government.

(EI, 91)

As regards India's poverty, he observes how the British had failed in their duty. He recounts meeting an American tourist in Lahore who could not get over India's misery. All he could say was: 'My God! *how long* did you say you have been running this country? Is this the best you can do? I had no idea — no idea at all — when I was in America!' (EI, 89) As a young man Thompson could see beauty and romance in India, but now it is different:

Yet today I seem to be able to see only India's poverty, ignorance, misery. I simply cannot understand how as a young man I saw romance and beauty there. I feel this so strongly that I have longed to have done with India for the few years that may be left to me, and have hoped that I should never write another book about it, except some historical work.

(EI, 90)

He recalls how Nehru pleaded with him: 'Please do not take away all this bitterness against my unhappy country!' (EI, 90) His answer was: 'I felt no bitterness against India. But I did feel bitterness against the sores which cover its surface and the wretchedness with which its beauty crawls.' (EI, 90) Then with great candour, he dismisses all the glib talk of the British work in India as highly exaggerated:

We ought to realise how the world feels about us and our work in India when it sees India's degradation and poverty. We give ourselves more bouquets than we deserve. We talk much of what we have done for India. . . . And her poverty remains dire and terrible. I believe that India is getting steadily poorer, and that I could prove this. The problem has got beyond us, and we have got to hand it over to Indians themselves.

(EI, 90)

Despite his sympathy and understanding of Indian politics, Thompson failed to assess the force of Muslim aspirations in India, and he tended to under-estimate the strength of the Muslim League. Thompson shows his pro-Hindu and pro-Congress bias in rejecting the Muslim League as the sole representative of the Indian Muslims. Thompson also shows his limitations in supposing that the real conflict between Hindus and Muslims was economic rather than religious.[11]
Coming to other minorities beside Muslims, he particularly

considers the difficulties faced by the domiciled or 'Anglo-Indian' community in a changing India. He does not think that any safeguards are necessary for them; their future lies with the Indian people. What in fact is needed is an eradication of any feeling of racial superiority on the part of 'Anglo-Indians' or the British:

> No man is responsible for his birth, and the wretched and blood-riddled nonsense about the superiority of the white breed, of 'Aryan' or 'Nordic' blood – all this must go, and men and women be equal in man's sight as well as in God's. And when we rebuild India in partnership with its peoples we should remember the domiciled community.

(EI, 80)

On the whole, despite inconsistencies and contradictions, Thompson shows a final shift towards a liberal tendency in his views. At the end of this book he repeats: 'If Indians are good enough to die with us they are good enough to be trusted'; that Britain is persisting in a course which is 'ethically indefensible'; and he exhorts his compatriots to free India now: 'Why refuse it now? Cut away the leading strings from the freedom we say we are offering, and you will find Indian leaders neither pedantic nor unreasonable.' (EI, 120)

VIOLENT NATIONALISM: *A FAREWELL TO INDIA*

A Farewell to India, like the other two novels of his Indian trilogy, is more of a political treatise than fiction. It picks up the theme of the British dilemma whether to keep or leave India in the face of the rising nationalism that he introduces in *An Indian Day*[12] and now examines it further in the context of the strains which a changing India imposes on the British. It is now 1929. The novel is set in rural Bengal at Vishnugram, not far from Darjeeling. It opens with the annual prize distribution ceremony at the local *zila* (district) Government College where the Rev. Robert Alden, the protagonist of Thompson's Indian novels and a mask for himself, is the acting principal. The Indian headmaster's stereotyped report about the good discipline of the school is in ironical contrast to the violent political agitation that is fast enveloping India. Even as the report is being read, Alden is worrying about the nationalist student leader, president of the self-styled Independent Students' Association, whom he had earlier expelled from the college and who is still harassing him. It is this harassment around which the main plot of the novel revolves.

Alden, a believer in the doctrine of action, is obsessed with the idea of tracing the revolutionary student leader so that he can bring him to book. At the start of the summer vacation, he decides to seek the advice of his missionary friend John Findlay of the Kanthala Mission. On his way to Kanthala, Alden spends a day in Calcutta where, while walking through the Maidan, he becomes nostalgic about the Company's days in India: 'The pageant of an alien splendour, aloof and arrogant, as certain as ever Rome or Nineveh had been that it was established for ever, had passed over this land.'[13] He reflects over the present decline in the glory of the Raj; even the change during his stay in India has been enormous: 'He had witnessed it in its last days of power, already threatened, but by an opposition so feeble as to be almost absurd. . . . How frailly their protest broke against the granite of the Raj!' (FI, 40–1) Now things are no longer the same:

> Now those days had vanished so utterly that it was only by a hard effort of memory that he could see them as having ever been real. The boot was on the other leg. Education was on sufferance, an imperious and reckless Nationalism ruled the stage, jerking his students back and forth like puppets.
>
> (FI, 41–2)

Findlay, described much more fully in *An Indian Day*, is a saintly figure who has arrived at a personal reconciliation with India on a deeply spiritual level. His discovery of this love for India as well as his assimilation of Indian mystical modes of thought has been achieved through a painful process involving adjustment of his values and links with his own religion and compatriots. Having understood the all-inclusive philosophy of India which sees good and evil as aspects of the same reality, he begins to accept the Western doctrine of action and the Eastern doctrine of detachment as complementary rather than contradictory. However, the very fact that Findlay now lives in near isolation in remote Bengal shows the triumph of the doctrine of contemplation and raises the question as to whether his solution is a practical one or not.

Findlay has been greatly influenced by an Indian saint, Sadhu Jayananda, once a member of the ICS, who has renounced the world to live as a hermit. The Sadhu had been an active opponent of the government during the Hindu agitation against the partition of

Bengal, and though he still keeps in touch with the nationalist movement, he is now essentially intent on attaining his *nirvana*: 'He was dreaming of infinity, withdrawing from existence into union with the *Parmatma*, the Absolute, that unconditioned pulseless Silence over whose surface our brief lives flit and twitter for their imaginary hour.'[14] For Thompson, a person like Jayananda represents the best in the Indian mystical tradition. It may also be interesting to note the similarities between Jayananda and Kipling's Sir Purun Das who too renounces the world and tries to achieve a balance between action and contemplation.

Findlay is happy to see Alden and proposes a meeting with Sadhu Jayananda who, he thinks, might be helpful in tracing or reasoning with the revolutionaries creating trouble at the Vishnugram College. Alden, though sympathetic towards Indians in a paternalistic way, does not really understand the logic behind violent nationalism; he is even doubtful of the results of the meeting with the Sadhu. Indian mysticism and philosophic abstractions do not attract him; like many of Kipling's characters, he is concerned with solving India's social and economic problems rather than giving Indians the right of self-government:

> When what India needs is to keep her nose to facts, she's gone off into abstractions. We cut down the opium, and they get drunk on print. They'll be starting Women's Clubs next. When all the English rage was for Macaulayese, they bettered us at that. They're already beating us at this pseudo-psychology tosh that's running wild.
>
> (FI, 68)

And he goes on to refute that there is any analogy between Canada and India on the basis of the Durham report:

> Point out to them that their Hindus and Mohammedans aren't agreeing, even while they're still in the stage for sheer fun, drawing up imaginary constitutions for an imaginary United Indian Union. They'll reply by quoting from the Durham Report before Canada got self-government, to show that they can't possibly be in a worse mess than Canada was then, when French and British were ready to fly at each other. The thing that matters . . . is not that they're *like*

Canada on paper, but that they *are* going to cut one another's throats.

(FI, 68)

At Sadhu Jayananda's *ashram* (hermitage), they meet a young Indian nationalist, Dinabandhu, who stands for the new forces that are sweeping the country. As opposed to Jayananda or Gandhi, Dinabandhu does not believe that independence can be achieved through non-violence: 'He was out of patience with Gandhi's methods and with all who played with the notion of Dominion status. He would have India very India, one and indivisible and sovereign, no matter what blood it cost.' (FI, 75)

Alden and Dinabandhu get involved in a heated argument. 'What good is violence going to do you?' (FI, 78) Alden asks. 'What good did it do the Irish?' the Indian retorts. Alden continues, 'You can steer India into peaceful partnership with the rest of the Empire, or you can enter a path which you think has always led to independence and glory before – that of assassination and guerrilla warfare.' (FI, 79) Sneering at 'peaceful partnership', Dinabandhu replies, 'Better rivers of blood than a nation with its soul in chains!' And he adds: 'India has been subjugated by blood, she shall win freedom by blood. Do you think we are afraid of being shot down by your machine-guns?' (FI, 81)

Dinabandhu then suddenly leaves the *ashram*, and Findlay comments on Alden's ignorance of the changing mood of the time. 'But how far does he [Dinabandhu] count?' (FI, 82) Alden asks. The Sadhu replies, 'He counts a great deal – now.' Continuing, he says, 'You English never learn that the age has moved until it is too late' (FI, 83); that Gandhi cannot keep things non-violent much longer; and that he himself has refused to be drawn back into the 'riot and anger of Indian politics'. (FI, 88) Wistfully the Sadhu adds: 'I am as out of date and obsolete as you two fellows. We belong to an India that has gone out as completely as the India of John Company days.' (FI, 88–9)

In a way the Sadhu is sad at the change which has been brought about as a result of contact with the British; the baneful touch of Western materialism has spoiled India: 'You have a new India on the stage, one that has seen wealth and power and arrogance, and wants to have a hand in the game. You've shown us another world, that seems greedy and glowing and strong, that seems to have everything, that crowds life with possessions.' (FI, 90)

A sad and sober man, Alden returns to his college which now opens for the new academic year. He feels helpless against the nationalists whose arguments make no sense to him; he is now convinced that *bhuts* (ghosts) or *devatas* (gods) have taken possession of the people and that nothing can be done about it. Here Thompson comes close to Kipling's dark powers and Forster's Marabar caves; the *bhuts* represent the mysterious, irrational spirit of India:

> I am beginning to believe in *bhuts* – in something dull, stupid, brute, malignant, invulnerable, with feet that take hold of the very soil. And it's in league with other *bhuts*, that are not *bhuts* at all, but *devatas*, living in an upper air of dreams and enthusiasms. It's an unnatural alliance, but a powerful one.
>
> (FI, 119)

At an earlier point he confesses:

> I am beginning to think that there's something elemental in this land, that's in revolt against us. . . . I think the age from time to time, in one land or another, gets sick of a certain people, and gets rid of them. It isn't reason, it isn't even the sword, that kicks them out. It's the *bhuts*. They're doing it now with the English, all over the world, and most of all in India.
>
> (FI, 117)

This vision of an impersonal, elemental force directing the destiny of India, a recurrent theme in Thompson's fiction,[15] is suggestive of a strong influence of both Kipling and Forster.

In the meantime the nationalist agitation gains momentum with the arrival of Gandhi in the area. Alden's impression of Gandhi, like that of Thompson, is a mixed one. He finds his economics outdated, his history distorted, and his figure ruined by forces whose instrument he seemed to be. Yet, he is awed by Gandhi's cool detachment and charismatic power: 'The Spirit of God has used this man, and has nearly done with him . . . I know he's wrong, yet I daren't say he's wrong. Frankly, I don't understand what I've been watching in India during these last twenty years.' (FI, 144–5)

The worsening political situation takes a critical turn with the Congress's ultimatum for the grant of dominion status to India. There are strikes all over; the mood of students becomes defiant; and Hinduism in Vishnugram becomes more and more militant with the ugly appearance of the fanatical *suddhi* or 'purification' movement that sought to reclaim all converts back into the Hindu fold. A Hindu *sankirtan* (religious procession) halts outside the church striving to enrage Christians. Alden's blood boils as he reflects over the difference between the present and the past: 'Those had been days when the sahib was still a god, most of all in such a place as this jungly Kanthala. A red and wrathful visage at a door would have been enough to scatter an army drunk with patriotic fervour.' (FI, 162)

Alden's sense of failure both on a national and personal level deepens. 'My missionary career has been one long failure,' (FI, 191) he confesses; at another point he talks of having wasted twenty years 'in what Government wittily calls Education' (FI, 181). He is fed up with political abstractions, he has seen India's poverty from too close a quarter, he is exasperated by Gandhi's hymns to the cow, and he rejects the Round Table Conferences as useless:

> What is India's greatest need today? More leopards. And what does this bureaucratic, oppressive, heartless Government do about it? Nothing. No, worse than nothing. . . . I'm changing my views fast . . . I'm beginning to see that all this chatter about Dominion status and gradual, peaceful progression to self-determination is rot.
>
> (FI, 190)

Douglas, the principal of the college, returns from his furlough, and Alden is now completely free to pursue his own interests. Accidentally, he stumbles on some extremist nationalists including Dinabandhu at a half-ruined shrine of an old Englishman, Klemmon Sahib. Dinabandhu is furious at Alden's spying around and wants to kill him if he continues to be a nuisance. Alden too is sick and tired of this whole affair, and he tries to make peace with the terrorists through Sadhu Jayananda. The Sadhu has a message for him from Dinabandhu instructing Alden to leave India immediately if he wants to save his life. Alden is cut to the quick at this message for he feels that he too has a claim to India, and he bursts out against the nationalists with great anger:

> They talk about exploitation, about hordes of officials, about our debauching and drugging India against her will, about the heaviest taxation in the world — when they must know, unless they are as half-witted as they seem to be dishonest and disreputable, that India

is mainly a vast picturesque desert, and that her revenues are too
trivial to be worth pillage.

(FI, 239)

He goes on with his tirade against Indians for being ungrateful for all
the work done by the British:

> But the whole thing is the damnedest dishonesty the world has ever
> seen — the Indian screaming about the injustice of our growing tea
> and jute, where nothing grew before, and the British diehard
> puffing about our great gifts to the country.

(FI, 240)

From now on Alden feels increasingly lonely and sensitive to
currents of feeling both in his own and the Indian community; he and
his people seem to have lost their way; the students at the college
become completely unmanageable thanks to Gandhi; finally he
suffers a nervous breakdown. He is advised to go to England as soon as
fit for travel; he is not to return to India. While recuperating, Alden
becomes convinced of the truth of his *bhut* theory, and his sister-in-
law agrees with him:

> The whole matter is now in celestial hands — or domestic hands, if
> you like. The *bhuts* have got to thrash it out with the Spirit of the
> Age, whether India is to stay in the Empire or not.

(FI, 279)

And Alden, in what is reminiscent of Kipling's story 'The Bridge
Builders', visualises these elemental forces in assembly conspiring the
ousting of the British from India:

> They are all in conclave now. . . . Somewhere in the forest there's
> a Parliament, of Padalsini, Mother Ganges, Mother Indus, the
> *thakurs* of the forest trees, the *bhuts* of the wayside, the *devatas* of the
> upper and lower air. . . . While the Round Table confers, these
> will be conferring also. And the future will go, not by what the
> Round Table Conference decides, but by what Nikal Seyn and
> Padalsini decide.

(FI, 279–80)

Even his sceptical brother-in-law becomes a believer:

I think I know what you mean, and I think I agree. . . . this Indian job has ceased to be worth the infinite bother it has become, and all the hatred and lying and misery it brings along. They're not our race, they don't think our thoughts. Why the devil were we ever tied up with them, and sent revolving on the same wheel of destiny? I half believe the *bhuts* will decide that our time is up.

(FI, 280)

Finally Alden, with his family, sails for England, but his heart is still in India: 'I'll come back. Alive or dead. For, if I ever die in England, some P. & O. will carry a spook stowaway.' (FI, 287)

In the final novel of the trilogy, *An End of the Hours*, Alden returns to India after five years, not as a *bhut* but in person, to examine the impact of changing conditions on Christian missions. The time is now 1936– 7, for the novel, perhaps the most rambling of the whole trilogy, incorporates some of Thompson's experiences of his 1937 visit to India. The note of bitter sadness at the disintegration of not only the Raj but also of the British work and the spirit of good will between the two sides that one notices in the earlier novels becomes deeper. On a personal level, his own sense of failure in establishing an understanding or *rapprochement* between himself and the Indians heightens the melancholy pervading the novel. What further adds to the overall disappointment is his acknowledgement of the defeat of Christianity in India: 'We had thought of a calm, steady process which would make India Christian and England understanding and pitiful, and both of us wise and great.'[16] In his bitterness Alden even complains against God for unkindness: 'When a man has known a landscape as I have the one to which I am going, and has taken it into his blood and brain, God should allow him to abide in it for eternity.'[17]

As Alden journeys through India in search of healing and peace, he comes to Buddh Gaya and feels relief on having contact with the spiritual heritage of India. From now on he becomes conscious, as he does in earlier novels too, of the presence of an essential, permanent India which has decreed the fall of the British; they were merely an instrument of blind, cosmic forces that one cannot completely comprehend. The only question is whether the British connection has been of any value at all and whether it will become a part of Indian heritage or not. The Sadhu Jayananda affirms that the British connection has been valuable to India, particularly in the area of developing a national identity. This affirmation helps Alden to feel a bit better; he leaves India hopeful of its spiritual, if not political, future.[18]

CONCLUSION: DIVIDED SYMPATHIES

Thompson presents an interesting case of a writer with divided sympathies – he feels a dual pull towards the justice of the Indian cause and a deep sense of loyalty to his own people; this is mainly responsible for the many inconsistencies and contradictions that one encounters in his writings. Furthermore, there is a conflict of attitude between his fiction and non-fiction which further complicates an analysis of his reaction to the imperial idea.

Thompson's non-fiction, despite the contradictions, is relatively straightforward. Here there is a clear division between his pre-1940 and post-1940 writings. In the pre-1940 works, though sympathetic towards nationalists' demands for self-government, he does not think that India is ripe for even dominion status. He calls attention to the more urgent problems of India, particularly its social and communal evils such as child marriage, *suttee*, poverty, caste system, disease, Hindu–Muslim clashes and so on. He sees the need for the British presence that is justified by its work in India of which he feels proud. He is aware of the British excesses and crimes, but by the same token he expects Indians to recognise the benefits of the Raj. His *Reconstruction of India* is a vigorous defence of the Raj. It is through a dispassionate, objective understanding of both sides, Indian and British, something which he believes he is embarking upon in his work, that a *rapprochement* can be effected. For instance, in the preface to his *The Rise and Fulfilment of British Rule in India* (written jointly with G. T. Garratt) he declares:

> We have both had long and close connections with India, and friendships that have given us a feeling of a second nationality; but inevitably our first loyalty is to our own country, one of the last in which free and unregimented thinking is still possible. Yet love of England cannot blind us to the dangers which beset Western civilization, and we are convinced of the immense influence that India, called to a reinvigorated existence, could exert in solving these problems which now oppress the mind of man. We send out this book hoping that it will work for that understanding between the two countries which fate has linked so strongly together.[19]

After 1940 the rising tide of nationalism along with the war makes him see the historical inevitability of full freedom for India; he realises that the question whether India is fit for independence is irrelevant; and though the immense problem of poverty remains, he now advocates that power must be transferred immediately if Indians are not to be alienated forever. He is at the same time conscious of the British failure in India. He blames this failure as much on human limitations as on the deliberate distance that the British kept from the Indians.

Despite his keen political sensibility and an awareness of the Hindu social evils for the exposure of which he admired *Mother India*, Thompson adopts a pro-Congress and pro-Hindu stance in his political and historical writings. He undervalues the Muslim demand for Pakistan and scoffs at the two-nation theory, which demonstrates his limitations. This pro-Hindu attitude is perhaps explained by his personal contacts with Hindu leaders and stay in Hindu Bengal.

In his non-fictional writings, Thompson also makes a strong plea for Western understanding of Indian literature and languages. He deplores the British ignorance of such a rich literature which can truly lead to a better appreciation of the Indian mind. Such a cultural-approach can hopefully bring about a synthesis of what is best in the Eastern and Western traditions, particularly their spiritual and material values. This trend, he believes, can already be witnessed in men like Tagore.

His fiction, written almost entirely before 1940, gives a slightly different picture of Thompson's response to the Raj. Of course his views are still unmodified by the post-1940 experiences, but as compared to his non-fiction of the pre-1940 period, one notices a more conservative and emotional support of the imperial idea. He is aware that the Raj is in its twilight and knows the intensity of the nationalist sentiment on the issue, but he is at pains to demonstrate the foolishness of the whole argument for freedom. There is no reason in the nationalist case; Gandhi may be a saint but he is not much of a thinker; violence and bloodshed cannot be condoned in the name of a struggle for freedom; and what India needs is a strong benevolent rule that should give the masses a 'good administration' which the Raj is obviously doing. He has other arguments for the continuation of the British presence. The Raj is not only providing India with good government, it is finally coming to grips with its age-old problems through an introduction of modern reforms; it is slowly but surely changing the soul of India. However, what pains him is Indian

ingratitude in this regard. But that does not matter; this is the lot of
the white man, he seems to argue in Kiplingesque terms. Thus his
fiction shows a paternalistic attitude towards India; he seems to
believe in the imperial idea with all its attendant myths. In holding
these beliefs, Thompson is close to Kipling.

The other point which strongly emerges from his fiction is a deep
sense of failure of the West in facing the challenge of the elemental,
impersonal, and dark forces that India seems to embody. These are
precisely the dark powers that Kipling speaks of or the reality of India
that Forster's caves symbolise. Here Thompson is building a similar
argument. The white man, though bound to be vanquished by these
dark powers, must however take up the challenge and help put some
kind of order, however fragile, on this area of darkness. However,
what disappoints him so much is that the British have already given
up, they are behaving as if the battle has been lost. Hence the bitterness
which permeates his Indian trilogy.

The conflicting views about India and the Raj in his fiction and
non-fiction make it difficult to pass a final judgement on Thompson's
stand on the issue. If we go by chronology, it is quite clear that in the
end he opposed the continuation of the Raj though he never
suggested the complete severance of all ties with India. His fiction
presents an opposing, a more emotional view. I tend to believe that
the point of view that emerges in his novels is a better guide to
Thompson's innermost feelings rather than the logical deductions
that he arrives at in his historical or political prose. He remains a good
example of what most honest, sensitive, and sincere Englishmen felt
about the Empire in those twilight days of the Raj – a division of
sympathies.

4 George Orwell

After Kipling and Forster, Orwell is perhaps the most important writer on the Raj,[1] and though he is generally regarded to be in direct revolt against both Kipling and the Empire, the relationship between Orwell and Kipling is far more complex than has been suggested, and similarly his reaction to the Raj is also not one of simple hostility. One must not allow oneself to be carried away by Orwell's anti-imperial or anti-Kipling stance alone for this is not the whole story; in order to form a correct view of Orwell's reaction to the Raj one must look into the many contradictions and paradoxes in Orwell's personality,[2] especially his points of contact with rather than departure from Kipling.

To begin with, Orwell, like Kipling, was a child of the Raj. Orwell was born at Motihari, Bengal in 1903 where his father worked in the Opium Department of the Indian Civil Service. His paternal grandfather had served in the Indian Army while his maternal grandfather had been a teak merchant in Burma. Like Kipling he too was sent to England at a very early age for education, had an unhappy childhood, and went to public schools[3] which imbued him with an enthusiasm for the Raj, respect for authority, belief in discipline and action, and all that is loosely termed the public-school spirit. In 1922, after graduation from Eton, Orwell joined the Indian Imperial Police and was trained in Burma. He served there for nearly five years and then in 1927, while home on leave, resigned from the service.

Orwell's first twenty-four years thus fall into a well-established pattern of training for membership in the *sahib* class of imperialist Britain. In fact, till this point, his career sounds more orthodox than that of Kipling, who never joined the machinery of the Raj in any official capacity. Moreover, the interesting question, as raised by Francis Odle, is not that Orwell decided on the East as a starting place for a career (for that was quite normal in those days), but that he chose to join the police rather than some branch of civil administration.[4] Apart from his family ties with Burma, which he cites as the reason for his choice, I believe that the aggressive public school spirit and a

romantic dream of becoming an empire-builder in a remote part of
the world had a great deal to do with his opting for the police service
in Burma.[5] It is thus no accident that he considered Kipling's poem
'Mandalay' as the finest poem in the English language,[6] and as Maung
Htin Aung remarks,[7] it is most likely that Orwell particularly
remembered the following lines:

> By the old Moulmein Pagoda, lookin' eastward to the sea,
> There's a Burma girl a-settin', an' I know she thinks o' me;
> For the wind's in the palm-trees, an' the temple-bells they say:
> 'Come you back, you British soldier; come you back to
>   Mandalay!'
>
> (DE, 418)

Another point worth noticing is that while he was thoroughly
disillusioned by Burma and his job that made him see the dirty work
of the Raj at close quarters, he was quite an efficient police officer and
he took his duties seriously — his duties involved detective work,
prison administration, and maintenance of general law and order. In
fact, at that time one could not see any trace of liberalism in Orwell.
For instance, Christopher Hollis, who met Orwell in Rangoon in
1925, recalls their conversation:

> We had a long talk and argument. In the side of him which he
> revealed to me at that time there was no trace of liberal opinions.
> He was at pains to be the imperial policeman, explaining that the
> theories of no punishment and no beating were all very well at
> public schools but that they did not work with the Burmese — in
> fact
> > Libbaty's a kind o' thing
> > Thet don't agree with niggers.[8]

Similarly Roger Beadon, a fellow police officer in Burma, tells us that
Orwell resigned from the police because of a rift with his boss rather
than any pangs of conscience.[9] Perhaps this is an extreme view, for
Orwell's reaction against his job and the Raj was not a total hoax;
perhaps his conflict remained entirely internal while he was in Burma.
However, the question of the degree and consistency of this reaction
is an open issue, for despite all his guilt complex engendered by his
experiences in Burma, he never really hated the Raj in the way he
recoiled from communism or fascism. Indeed, at times he even

admired the Raj. Moreover, one must not ignore the fact that his life in Burma was a life of action, and he never dismissed the public school virtues as useless. This belief in duty and action further link him with Kipling. As his friend Malcolm Muggeridge has remarked, there was a strong Kiplingesque side to Orwell's personality which made him romanticise the Raj occasionally. Muggeridge also records that whenever he told Orwell that he and Kipling had a great deal in common, he would laugh and change the subject but never denied it.[10]

Orwell had a great admiration for Kipling; he came under his spell quite early in life. Thus he speaks of Kipling as 'the story-teller who was so important to my childhood'.[11] In his note on Kipling's death in 1936, Orwell wrote:

> He was a sort of household god with whom one grew up and whom one took for granted whether one liked him or whether one did not. For my own part I worshipped Kipling at thirteen, loathed him at seventeen, enjoyed him at twenty, despised him at twenty-five, and now again rather admire him.
>
> (I, 183)

It is true that this admiration is mingled with a criticism of some of the content of Kipling's writings, but Orwell's attitude towards Kipling is never denigratory. Often his attack on Kipling ends up as a defence of Kipling — his well-known essay 'Rudyard Kipling' (1942) is a case in point. Let us take a closer look at this essay.

Orwell begins by finding fault with Eliot's apology for Kipling's barbarity and imperialism, charging Eliot with 'defending Kipling where he is not defensible' (II, 215); he declares that one should condemn Kipling for his vices: 'Kipling is a jingo imperialist, he is morally insensitive and aesthetically disgusting.' (II, 215) However, after having lured the reader by calling Kipling a few names, he devotes the rest of the essay to a vigorous defence of Kipling, doing exactly what he said should not have been attempted by Eliot.

First of all, he draws a distinction between imperialism and fascism and refutes the charge that Kipling had fascist tendencies. Far from being a fascist, Kipling was, he declares, 'the most humane or the most "progressive" a person is able to be nowadays' (II, 215). He shows how anti-Kipling views are often based on prejudice, misunderstanding or use of his words out of their proper context. He illustrates this point by referring to the notorious line 'lesser breeds without the

Law' from 'Recessional'. It is generally assumed that the 'lesser breeds' are 'natives', and 'a mental picture is called up of some pukka sahib in a pith helmet kicking a coolie' (II, 216), but in its context, Orwell argues, the sense of the line is almost the exact opposite of this. The phrase 'lesser breeds' refers to the Germans who were 'without the Law' in the sense of being lawless, not in the sense of being powerless, and he goes on to state: 'The whole poem, conventionally thought of as an orgy of boasting, is a denunciation of power politics, British as well as German.' (II, 216) As a further proof of his statement, he calls attention to the Biblical language and the deep note of humility of 'Recessional'.

After proving that Kipling cannot be accused of fascism, he makes an interesting defence of his imperialism not by denying it but by setting up another fine distinction between modern imperialism and the nineteenth-century imperialism. In other words, he makes a plea for judging Kipling in a proper historical context. The pre-1914 imperialism, as opposed to the modern 'gangster outlook', could be romantic and gentlemanly despite all its faults:

> The imperialism of the eighties and nineties was sentimental, ignorant and dangerous, but it was not entirely despicable. The picture then called up by the word 'empire' was a picture of overworked officials and frontier skirmishes, not of Lord Beaverbrook and Australian butter. It was still possible to be an imperialist and a gentleman, and of Kipling's *personal* decency there can be no doubt.
>
> (I, 183—4)

He realises that Kipling had his limitations. For instance, Kipling does not understand that 'an empire is primarily a money-making concern' and that 'the map is painted red chiefly in order that the coolie may be exploited'; Kipling sees imperialism as a sort of 'forcible evangelizing': 'You turn a Gatling gun on a mob of unarmed "natives", and then you establish "the Law", which includes roads, railways and a court-house.' (II, 217)

However, despite an ignorance of the economics of imperialism, Kipling, Orwell points out, saw that the British were at least people who did things; hence his admiration for the administrators, soldiers, and engineers. Orwell goes on to comment:

It may be that all that they did was evil, but they changed the face of the earth (it is instructive to look at a map of Asia and compare the railway system of India with that of the surrounding countries), whereas they could have achieved nothing, could not have maintained themselves in power for a single week, if the normal Anglo-Indian outlook had been that of, say, E. M. Forster.

(II, 219)

This is a very revealing statement from someone who is supposed to be such a great opponent of the Raj. Here we have a categorical defence of the Raj on the basis of the British work in India and elsewhere. It is also instructive to note his rejection of Forster's portrayal of 'Anglo-Indian' society as highly exaggerated or false. On the other hand, Kipling's picture of India is credited to be true — Kipling is our only chronicler of nineteenth-century Anglo-India, he declares with justification.

Orwell also points out that despite his championship of the Empire, Kipling is perhaps one of the most severe critics of Britain and the *sahibs* who ran the magnificent machinery of the Raj. In fact, he was never one of them; he mixed with 'the wrong' people; he was never approved of by 'Anglo-Indians'. Kipling's integrity, realism, and a high sense of responsibility are thus further grounds of Orwell's admiration for him. He admits that Kipling sold out to the British governing class, not financially but emotionally, and this warped his political judgement. However, he 'gained the advantage of having at least tried to imagine what action and responsibility are like'. (II, 229)

Orwell thus comes out as an admirer of Kipling though at the start he gave the impression that he was going to tear him apart. The point I am trying to make is that Orwell's reaction to the imperial idea and Kipling is complex — it is not one of simple condemnation or adulation. This attitude fits well with the many contradictions and paradoxes that characterise Orwell — the split between Blair and Orwell is an indication of the deep conflict within him. Perhaps while the conservative Blair tended to admire Kipling and the Raj, the liberal Orwell rejected them — the dilemma was never really resolved. Here again one can see a close parallel with Kipling's ambivalent attitude towards India and the Raj that is projected through *Kim*:

Something I owe to the soil that grew —
More to the life that fed —
But most to Allah Who gave me two
Separate sides to my head.

(XIX, 214)

APPROACHES TO THE RAJ: NON-FICTION

Orwell is perhaps one of the most highly politicised writers of this
century; almost whatever he wrote was motivated by political or
social concern; he was primarily a social and political activist and only
secondarily an artist. His strength lay in a keen sense of observation
and ability to describe things; his work is thus stamped by a fidelity to
experience and is closely related to the historical events or political
issues of his time. There is thus not much of a division between his
fiction and non-fiction; his fiction also borders on the factual, and as
Raymond Williams has observed, the unity of Orwell's 'documen-
tary' and 'imaginative' writing is the very first thing one notices.[12] In
other words, a study of his non-fiction is as important as of his fiction
for an understanding of Orwell's ideas.

As regards politics, Orwell's major concern is with socialism,
communism, and fascism. The number of his essays or other non-
fiction dealing with imperialism is relatively small, which is perhaps
an indication of his mixed attitude to the Raj.[13] Among these the
most significant pieces are 'A Hanging' (1931), 'Shooting an
Elephant' (1936), portions of *The Road to Wigan Pier* (1937), 'Not
Counting Niggers' (1939) and 'Marrakech' (1939). Let us take a
closer look at these writings.

I will first take up *The Road to Wigan Pier* where in Chapter 9 we
have a detailed account of his reaction to the Raj. Orwell begins with
pointing out that the real enthusiasm for the Empire for him and the
entire shabby-genteel class to which he belonged derived from the
fact that in India or other parts of the Empire, an Englishman could
afford a lifestyle not possible at home; he could live there like a
gentleman with power and prestige. However, after five years of
membership in this shabby-genteel *sahib* class in British-occupied
Burma, Orwell had enough, for he came to recognise the dirty work
of the Raj: 'I was in the Indian Police five years, and by the end of that
time I hated imperialism. I was serving with a bitterness which I
probably cannot make clear. In the free air of England that kind of

thing is not fully intelligible. In order to hate imperialism you have got to be part of it.'[14]

And he was not the only person who developed this hatred of the Raj; the majority of 'Anglo-Indians', he says, were not complacent about their role and position. Even the thickest-skinned 'Anglo-Indian', Orwell remarks, was aware of the tyranny of the system he was serving, but he could not do anything about it — they all felt that they were in a trap and might as well make the best of it. 'Of course we've no right in this blasted country at all. Only now we're here for God's sake let's stay here,' was the comment that one heard constantly in the colonies. The truth is, Orwell goes on to argue, that foreign oppression cannot be justified in any way, even on the supposed basis of service and development work; that the British would fight to the last man sooner than be ruled by Chinamen; and that it is wrong to go and lord it in a foreign country where you are not wanted.

As a natural result of serving this tyrannical system, every 'Anglo-Indian' was haunted by 'a sense of guilt' which he could not express openly for there was no freedom of speech. Hence at the first safe opportunity, their hidden bitterness overflowed. He recalls meeting on a train journey an Englishman from the Education Department whose name he never asked. They spent the whole night in pitch-black darkness cursing the Raj: 'We damned the British Empire — damned it from the inside, intelligently and intimately. It did us both good. But we had been speaking forbidden things, and in the haggard morning light when the train crawled into Mandalay, we parted as guilty as any adulterous couple.' (RW, 127)

Orwell developed a particularly 'bad conscience' because he was doing the hangman's job: 'But I was in the police, which is to say that I was part of the actual machinery of despotism. Moreover, in the police you see the dirty work of Empire at close quarters.' (RW, 127) Other 'Anglo-Indians' such as engineers, doctors, or forest officers could rationalise their presence by playing the role of benevolent despots; but Orwell could not do so because of the nature of his work. He remembers how an American missionary who came to see him at the police station when some suspects were being questioned said to him, 'I wouldn't care to have your job.' That made him horribly ashamed: 'So *that* was the kind of job I had! Even an ass of an American missionary, a teetotal cock-virgin from the Middle West, had the right to look down on me and pity me!' (RW, 128)

His job also made him see the injustice and inhumanity of the British judicial system:

> Our criminal law . . . is a horrible thing. It needs very insensitive
> people to administer it. The wretched prisoner squatting in the
> reeking cages of the lock-ups, the grey cowed faces of the long-
> term convicts, the scarred buttocks of the men who had been
> flogged with bamboos, the women and children howling when
> their menfolk were led away under arrest – things like these are
> beyond bearing when you are in any way directly responsible for
> them.
>
> (RW, 128)

He often felt that he was the real criminal – 'I never went into a jail
without feeling (most visitors to jails feel the same) that my place
was on the other side of the bar.' (RW, 128)

His sense of guilt and repulsion at British justice comes out sharply
in an early essay, 'A Hanging'. Here with stark realism he describes a
hanging scene in Burma. The ritualistic way in which the execution is
carried out is designed to lend it a mechanical, non-human aspect
which helps in mitigating responsibility for this terrible job. The
condemned man is handled, not as a human being, but as 'a fish which
is still alive and may jump back into the water' (I, 67). The anonymity
of the prisoner and hangman (a fellow prisoner who further helps in
relieving the authorities of responsibility for the killing) also contrib-
utes to the impersonality of this hanging. What is ironical is that the
essential humanity of the condemned man who is continuously seen in
non-human terms, is recognised by a dog who interrupts the
procession to the gallows. And suddenly Orwell sees 'the unspeakable
wrongness, of cutting a life short when it is in full tide' (I, 68).

It was these experiences that later led him to oppose capital
punishment. For a while he worked out an anarchistic theory that all
government is evil, that punishment does more harm than good,
though afterwards he realised that 'it is always necessary to protect
peaceful people from violence. In any state of society where crime can
be profitable you have got to have a harsh criminal law and
administer it ruthlessly; the alternative is Al Capone.' (RW, 128)
Nevertheless, he continued to plead for the abolition of hanging as a
form of capital punishment:

> It is not a good symptom that hanging should still be the accepted
> form of capital punishment in this country. Hanging is a barbarous,
> inefficient way of killing anybody, and at least one fact about it –

quite widely known, I believe – is so obscene as to be almost unprintable.

(IV, 279)

The bad conscience and guilt complex made him leave the police for he felt that he had to expiate his sins. He reduced everything to the simple theory that the oppressed are always right and the oppressors are always wrong (later he modified his stand) and felt that he had got to escape not merely from imperialism but from every form of man's dominion over man. So in expiation for his guilt he went slumming in Paris and London; he could not identify himself with the natives in Burma, but at home he could mix with the poor who had a lot in common with the oppressed Burmese.

The other attack that he levels against imperialism is on economic grounds which he believes is often hypocritically ignored. For example in his essay 'Not Counting Niggers', Orwell exposes the hypocrisy of a proposal for the union of democratic countries as a deterrent to communism – to call the British and French Empires democracies, he declares, is preposterous for these Empires are essentially a mechanism for exploiting cheap coloured labour:

It is not in Hitler's power, for instance, to make a penny an hour a normal industrial wage; it is perfectly normal in India, and we are at great pains to keep it so. One gets some idea of the real relationship of England and India when one reflects that the *per capita* annual income in England is something over £80, and in India about £7. It is quite common for an Indian coolie's leg to be thinner than the average Englishman's arm. And there is nothing racial in this, for well-fed members of the same races are of normal physique; it is due to simple starvation. This is the system which we all live on and which we denounce when there seems to be no danger of its being altered.

(I, 437)

In another short essay, 'Marrakech', he notes some of the effects of French exploitation of Morocco. All around one sees thousands of emaciated brown people in rags; it is difficult to believe that one is walking among human beings. This is the story of all colonial empires; the colonial process tends to reduce natives to a sub-human level. 'What does Morocco mean to a Frenchman?' he asks. 'Perhaps an orange-grove or a job in government service,' and he goes on to

add: 'One could probably live here for years without noticing that for
nine tenths of the people the reality of life is an endless, back-breaking
struggle to wriggle a little food out of an eroded soil.' (I, 429– 30)
After painting a moving picture of Moroccan poverty for which he
holds the French responsible, he turns his attention to a shy young
negro soldier who gives him a look of profound respect for 'he has
been taught that the white race are his masters, and he still believes it'.
However, the question is how long can this myth go on:

> But there is one thought which every white man (and in this
> connexion it doesn't matter two pence if he calls himself a Socialist)
> thinks when he sees a black army marching past. 'How much
> longer can we go on kidding these people? How long before they
> turn their guns in the other direction?'
>
> (I, 432)

Despite such a clear understanding of the horrible process of
imperialism which is destructive for the oppressed and the oppressor,
Orwell, true to his Lord Jim syndrome, is torn between a hatred of
colonialism and hatred of the colonised. His well-known essay,
'Shooting an Elephant', is a case in point. While he despised the
Imperial Police and the whole oppressive system it stood for, he was
enraged against 'the evil-spirited little beasts' who tried to make his
job impossible; while he revolted against 'the dirty work of Empire',
he thought that 'the greatest joy in the world would be to drive a
bayonet into a Buddhist priest's guts'. (I, 266)
In this essay Orwell describes how when he was in Moulmein as a
police officer, he had to reluctantly shoot a runaway work elephant
who had gone 'must'. He did not want to kill it, for a working
elephant was very valuable, and secondly he knew that the elephant
was not really wild. However, by the time he approached the
elephant, a seething crowd of excited, grinning Burmese eager to
have a bit of fun and meat, had gathered around him. They expected
him to kill the elephant; he could feel the pressure of their collective
will and had no choice:

> And it was at this moment, as I stood there with the rifle in my
> hands, that I first grasped the hollowness, the futility of the white
> man's dominion in the East. Here was I, the white man with his
> gun, standing in front of the unarmed native crowd – seemingly
> the leading actor of the piece; but in reality I was only an absurd

puppet pushed to and fro by the will of those yellow faces behind. I perceived in this moment that when a white man turns tyrant it is his own freedom that he destroys. He becomes a sort of hollow, posing dummy, the conventionalized figure of a sahib.

(I, 269)

In order to keep up the prestige of the British occupation, he had to act like a *sahib* – to appear resolute, to know his own mind, and do definite things. So, much against his will, he shot the elephant. The elephant sagged flabbily to its knees in great agony, dying a slow death. One can read this story as a parable of the Raj – the dying elephant being symbolic of the dying Empire. The empire-builder is often forced to act in certain ways, not because he wants to, but because he is expected to behave like a *sahib*. The power of the white man is thus an illusion; the *sahib* loses his own freedom through the tyranny he imposes on others. The process of colonisation is thus self-destructive.

This incident offers an interesting parallel and contrast to Kipling's story 'Naboth', termed by the author 'an allegory of Empire'. Here an Indian, taking advantage of an Englishman's hospitality and protection, sets up a shop on his benefactor's property and grows prosperous. Although his growing business puts limits on the Englishman's freedom, nothing can be done about it. Finally, someone gets killed because of the actions of the Indian, and this leads to his expulsion from the Englishman's premises. It is apparent that Kipling is writing about two peoples, not two individuals. The similarity here, as pointed out by Allen Greenberger, is that often the Englishman has to act in a way he does not want to.[15] However, there is also a difference between Orwell's story and that of Kipling. Kipling's Englishman finally gets rid of the Indian and asserts his will, whereas Orwell's protagonist has to submit himself to the will of the natives. This difference gives an indication of the extent to which the Raj had declined from the self-confidence of Kipling's days.

REALITY OF THE RAJ: *BURMESE DAYS*

Orwell's first novel, *Burmese Days* (1934), though generally underestimated, is remarkable in many ways. It gives the key to much of Orwell's later writings, showing his strengths and weaknesses, contradictions and paradoxes. Artistically too the novel is quite successful – here Orwell appears very much concerned with structure, character, texture, and in the possibilities of the form itself.[16] And last but not least, it is one of the best post-Kipling treatments of the Raj.

The socio-political aspect is primary to the novel; it was certainly written as part of his expiation of the enormous guilt he had developed while in the employ of the Raj. The political purpose, as Orwell states in 'Why I Write', was always uppermost in his mind, and his constant problem was how to fuse politics and art into one whole – something he thought he finally achieved in *Animal Farm*. What distinguishes *Burmese Days* from his other writings is precisely this fusion of political and artistic purposes; it is not a simplistic description of the Raj, but an intricate study of the moral and psychological impact of imperialism on the people who are forced to live in a colonial context.

In *Burmese Days* Orwell is attempting something similar to E. M. Forster's *A Passage to India*, though his performance is not equally impressive. It is very likely that Orwell was influenced by *A Passage to India*, which appeared in 1924, when he was still serving in Burma. And there are obvious parallels between the two novels. As pointed out by Jeffrey Meyers,[17] both novels deal with the lack of communication between diverse races, particularly the British and Asians; the difficulties of friendship between an Englishman and an Indian doctor under conditions imposed by the Raj; and an English girl who comes to the colonies in search of a husband. Both novels use extensive club scenes in order to expose the bigotry and racism of the 'Anglo-Indian' society, and both end on a bleak note, though Orwell's book is far more pessimistic than Forster's. The similarities in fact go much deeper. Like Forster (and Kipling), Orwell is also concerned with understanding the nature of the dark powers symbolised by India or Burma; it is within this larger philosophical context that the political theme is woven; this is how Orwell endeavours to fuse politics into art.

Burma, like India in Kipling's and Forster's Indian works, is thus one of the main characters in *Burmese Days*, and it has all the familiar features associated with the all-powerful, sinister, mysterious goddess called India. In fact, Burma appears to be an extension, though on a smaller scale, of the essential India that we recognise in the Hindu gods of Kipling's stories, the hustle and bustle of the Grand Trunk Road in *Kim* or the Marabar caves in *A Passage to India*. It is presented as a terrifying dark power which is simultaneously repulsive and attractive and which never leaves hold of one. Even when Orwell had left Burma, it continued to haunt him. In *The Road to Wigan Pier* he remarks that 'the landscapes of Burma, which, when I was among them, so appalled me as to assume the qualities of a nightmare, afterward stayed so hauntingly in my mind that I was obliged to write a novel about them to get rid of them' (RW, 129). The landscape, which figures so heavily in the novel, is more symbolic than literal, expressing the very spirit of hostile Burma:

> By the roadside, just before you got to the jail, the fragments of a stone pagoda were littered, cracked and overthrown by the strong roots of a peepul tree. The angry carved faces of demons looked up from the grass where they had fallen. Nearby another peepul tree had turned round a palm, uprooting it and bending it backwards in a wrestle that had lasted a decade.[18]

Here it is interesting to note the images of death, decay, and destruction which normally characterise the Burmese landscape. Beyond the ruined temple there was a cemetery: 'The creeping jasmine, with tiny orange-hearted flowers, had over-grown everything. Among the jasmine, large rat-holes led down into the graves.' (BD, 227) And hungry vultures constantly hover on the scene, indicating the malignant nature of the entity called Burma; the overall atmosphere is suffocating and stifling:

> It was only half-past eight, but the month was April, and there was a closeness in the air, a threat of the long, stifling midday hours. Occasional faint breaths of wind, seeming cool by contrast, stirred the newly drenched orchids that hung from the eaves. Beyond the orchids one could see the dusty, curved trunk of a palm tree, and then the blazing ultramarine sky. Up in the zenith, so high that it dazzled one to look at them, a few vultures circled without the quiver of a wing.
>
> (BD, 5)

The all-encompassing jungle is the dominating landscape which is an appropriate metaphor for the reality represented by Burma:

> Whichever way one looked one's view was shut in by the multitudinous ranks of trees, and the tangled bushes and creepers that struggled round their bases like the sea round the piles of a pier.

It was so dense, like a bramble bush extending mile after mile, that one's eyes were oppressed by it. Some of the creepers were huge, like serpents.

(BD, 157)

For the most part, the jungle is unpleasant, wild, unexplored, and dangerous. However, it has an attractive side to it as well — it can be pleasant and beautiful; its flowers, greenery, and wild life bring out this aspect. Its lovely imperial green pigeons are among the most charming birds in Asia; its tigers and leopards are of dazzling beauty; and even its wild cocks are graceful.

The dual nature of Burma manifests itself in other ways, for example in the bazaar scenes of Kyauktada. Reminiscent of the colourful scenes in *Kim*, Orwell's pictures of the native bazaar are equally suggestive of squalor and beauty:

The bazaar was an enclosure like a very large cattle pen, with low stalls, mostly palm-thatched, round its edge. In the enclosure, a mob of people seethed, shouting and jostling; the confusion of their multi-coloured clothes was like a cascade of hundreds-and-thousands poured out of a jar.

(BD, 119)

Perhaps the whole enigmatic spirit of Burma, at once terrifying and irrisistible, is most effectively summed up in the figure of a *pwe* dancer:

'Just look at that girl's movement. . . . It's grotesque, it's even ugly, with a sort of wilful ugliness. And there's something sinister in it too. There's a touch of the diabolical in all Mongols. And yet when you look closely, what art, what centuries of culture you can see behind it! . . . In some way that I can't define to you, the whole life and spirit of Burma is summed up in the way that girl twists her arms.'

(BD, 100)

It must however be acknowledged that the emphasis is on the ugly or sinister aspect of Burma. This may be seen in the character of U Po Kyin, the Burmese sub-divisional magistrate of Kyauktada. He is a thoroughly evil, scheming man who has risen to his present position through blackmail, bribery, and an acute understanding of British hypocrisy. His ruling passion is to control others while remaining in the background, and he admirably succeeds in this aim because he knows the weaknesses of both Asians and British. U Po Kyin manipulates all, including the glorious *sahibs*, like puppets; he seems to be an assertion of the point which Orwell made earlier in 'Shooting an Elephant', that when the white man turns tyrant it is his own freedom he destroys; that in a colonial context the white man only has an illusion of power. U Po Kyin is thus an embodiment of the destructive power of Burma, and he is appropriately associated with a crocodile.

The opposing force in Burma is the British Raj represented by the handful of 'Anglo-Indians' in the remote outpost of Kyauktada. By being an opponent of the dark powers symbolised by Burma, it does not necessarily imply that the Raj is an agent of good powers – Orwell does not see the conflict between Burma and the Raj as a simple conflict of evil and good. The two forces in fact seem to have a great deal in common, particularly their destructive abilities. The Raj, in this power struggle, seems to have made some gains; but its real control does not extend beyond the local jail, courthouse, police-station, and the European club. Moreover, it is questionable as to how long even this semblance of control will last.

The British who seek refuge in the sanctuary of their Kipling-haunted club define the essential character of the Raj. The first thing that one notices about them is that they are all seen in animal terms which link them with the crocodile-like U Po Kyin and the Burmese jungle. As noted by Robert A. Lee, the bestial pattern runs throughout the book.[19] Mr Macgregor, the deputy commissioner, reminds one of a turtle; Ellis, a timber manager, is goatish; Mrs Lackersteen and her niece Elizabeth are lizard-like; Maxwell, the forest ranger, is like a carthorse colt; Verrall, the army officer, is a combination of the buffalo and the leopard; and Flory, the central character of the novel, is like a cur or a dog. And these animal images are associated with the overt characteristics of all these persons. Thus there is a definite suggestion that these people are all savages, that there is no difference between them and the beasts of the jungle, and that this is what happens if one lives in a totalitarian or colonial society.

The inhuman side of the English can be seen in their narrow-minded racist attitudes. Idling in the seeming security of their citadel-like club, they indulge in drink, gossip, scandal-mongering, and petty talk that veers round the same subject: ' . . . the insolence of the natives, the supineness of the Government, the dear dead days, when the British Raj *was* the British Raj and please give the bearer fifteen lashes' (BD, 33). Here are such people as Macgregor, who stiffens at the word 'nigger' and is quite fond of the natives 'provided they were given no freedom' (BD, 29). Westfield, the deputy superintendent of police, is constantly regretting that he cannot shoot some natives at will – 'It's all law and order that's done for us.' (BD, 31) Mrs Lackersteen is upset over the corroding authority of the Raj: 'We seem to have no *authority* over the natives nowadays, with all these dreadful reforms.' (BD, 28) And Ellis longs for a General Dyer to put the 'beggars' in their place: 'We could all put things right in a month if we chose. It only needs a pennyworth of pluck. Look at Amritsar. Look how they caved in after that. Dyer knew the stuff to give them.' (BD, 31)

The one Englishman who feels sick and tired of both the Raj and the racism of his fellow-countrymen is Flory, a lonely timber merchant, who has been in Burma for fifteen years. Cursed by a hideous birthmark on his cheek that sets him apart as a marked man, Flory tries to maintain civilised and humane values in the face of heavy odds. He has already gone 'native' to a certain extent, has 'bolshie' views, takes a lively interest in the local people and culture, and is on intimate terms with an Indian doctor, Veraswami, superintendent of the local jail.

Flory's friendship with Dr Veraswami arouses the wrath of other 'Anglo-Indians', for the club is now required to desegregate itself by electing a non-white member, and as the highest Asian official in town, Dr Veraswami is the obvious choice. They are all determined to keep the 'nigger' out; Ellis, who epitomises British racism, bullies Flory into not supporting the nomination of his Indian friend:

> I don't care if you choose to pal up with the scum of the bazaar. If it pleases you to go to Veraswami's house and drink whisky with all his nigger pals, that's your look out. Do what you like outside the Club. But, by God, it's a different matter when you talk of bringing niggers here. . . . By God, he'd go out with my boot behind him if I ever saw his black snout inside that door.
>
> (BD, 23)

Ellis continuously baits Flory with remarks about 'that little nigger Very-slimy' and reads him a snappish little sermon, taking as his text 'the five chief beatitudes of the pukka sahib', namely:

Keeping up your prestige,
The firm hand (without the velvet glove),
We white men must hang together,
Give them an inch and they'll take an ell, and
Esprit de Corps.

(BD, 181)

The action of the novel revolves around the question of the admission of a non-white into the club. As Maung Htin Aung tells us,[20] this issue puts the events of the novel in a specific historical and political context, the turbulent 1919–39 period when Anglo-Burmese relations were particularly tense. Burma was left out of the Government of India Act of 1919 which brought dyarchy and other reforms to India. The Burmese reacted with mass agitation spearheaded by monks and students – an event which is used in the novel in Ellis's clash with protesting schoolboys. Dyarchy reforms were ultimately extended to Burma in 1923, which included recruitment of natives into senior positions and desegregation of European clubs. The English thought that these were big concessions though these measures never satisfied the Burmese. They were bent upon complete freedom and there were many uprisings, especially in the countryside; British rule finally ended in 1948.

Rejected by his community, Flory sets himself up as its critic and bitterly attacks its fundamental values, particularly hypocrisy, racial bigotry, and imperialism. His argument is simple and reasonable. He denounces the Raj as a money-making machine, 'the British Empire is simply a device for giving trade monopolies to the English' (BD, 38); he rejects the hypocritical myth of the imperial mission: 'I'm here to make money, like everyone else. All I object to is the slimy white man's burden humbug. The pukka sahib pose. It's so boring' (BD, 37); he sees the immorality of all notions of racial supremacy symbolised by the exclusiveness of the club; the British have done nothing to uplift Indians: 'Look at our schools – factories for cheap clerks. We've never taught a single useful manual trade to the Indians. We daren't; frightened of the competition in industry' (BD, 39); and he believes that instead of bringing progress they are destroying native culture and civilisation: 'before we've finished we'll have wrecked the whole Burmese national culture. But we're not civilising them, we're only rubbing our dirt on to them.' (BD, 40) He is filled with hatred of the Raj and *pukka sahibs*:

In the end the secrecy of your revolt poisons you like a secret disease. Your whole life is a life of lies. Year after year you sit in Kipling-haunted little Clubs, whisky to right of you, *Pink 'un* to the left of you, listening and eagerly agreeing while Colonel Bodger develops his theory that these bloody Nationalists should be boiled in oil. You hear your Oriental friends called 'greasy little babus', and you admit, dutifully, that they *are* greasy little babus. You see louts fresh from school kicking grey-haired servants. The time comes when you burn with hatred of your own countrymen, when you long for a native rising to drown their Empire in blood.

                                                                    (BD, 66)

Flory thus expresses many of Orwell's own views on the Raj, but in the very act of denouncing the Raj, Flory exposes his essential weakness — he is not man enough to declare these sentiments before his countrymen; he does so only in private when he is with Dr Veraswami. What is more degrading is that he even betrays his friend by putting his signature to the notice rejecting the election of Dr Veraswami to the club: 'Flory had signed a public insult to his friend. He had done it for the same reason as he had done a thousand such things in his life; because he lacked the small spark of courage that was needed to refuse.' (BD, 61) He knows that he is a coward, and he also recognises that the 'stifling, stultifying world' of imperialism in which he lives has poisoned him for ever. Flory is a sick man — as sick as 'Pox Britannica' whom he refers to as an old patient of his friend, Dr Veraswami.

Ironically enough Dr Veraswami is a great defender of the Raj — something which raises the question of the value of Flory's relationship with him. When Flory condemns his own countrymen and the Raj, Veraswami protests vehemently: 'But truly, truly, Mr Flory, you must not speak so! Why iss it that always you are abusing the pukka sahibs, ass you call them? They are the salt of the earth. Consider the great things they have done — consider the great administrators who have made British India what it iss. Consider Clive, Warren Hastings, Dalhousie, Curzon.' (BD, 36) The Indian doctor is fanatically loyal to the British; he has implicit faith in all the myths underlying the imperial idea, including the belief that he, as an Indian, belonged to 'an inferior and degenerate race' (BD, 38).

David L. Kubal, in his perceptive study of the novel, remarks that both Veraswami and Flory, in view of their ideas and attitudes, are isolated from their own races, yet, ironically, also separated from one another; this indicates that imperialism never unifies but always separates man from man.[21] This may be so. But the point remains that despite their differences, Flory and Veraswami are friends, and secondly, Veraswami, in spite of his nauseating obsequiousness, is presented as a good, honest man whose sincerity is genuine. Given Orwell's contradictions and paradoxes, it is possible to see in Veraswami Orwell's hidden sympathy for the Raj and his recognition of the positive aspect of the Empire. Coming from the mouth of an educated Indian, no matter how big a turncoat or toady he may be, this admiration for the Raj has a certain weight. Moreover, Veraswami is not a hoax; he is certainly typical of those few Indians who were fortunate to enter the coveted civil service and who served the Raj with unflinching loyalty. The very fact that Veraswami is not portrayed as evil or loathsome (while almost all other Asians in the novel tend to be evil) indicates that his view, however distorted, should be listened to. Perhaps Orwell is suggesting that behind all those myths such as white man's burden or the public-school spirit there is some iota of truth.

Flory's hesitation in openly supporting the admission of Veraswami to the club is further complicated by two factors. First, U Po Kyin is engaged in a conspiracy of blackmail against the Indian doctor and his friends, including Flory, in his bid to prevent Veraswami's admission to the *nirvana* represented by the club. Secondly, and more importantly, Flory falls in love with a newly-arrived English girl in Kyauktada who wants him to behave as a *pukka sahib*.

Elizabeth Lackersteen has the makings of a typical *memsahib*. She loathes art and culture; firmly believes in the Raj and her racial superiority; and is ruthlessly looking for a suitable husband. Flory immediately falls for her and even abandons his Burmese mistress for her sake. But they fail to understand each other; Flory's efforts in interesting her in the native world of colourful bazaars and ceremonial *pwe* dances only result in an ever-increasing estrangement between them. Mentally and spiritually they are poles apart; she only warms to him when he can talk or act like a *sahib*. For example, it is during the tiger-shoot that she decides to accept him; the hunt and the smell of blood bring them together; this is a subtle comment on the big game of the Raj itself — the colonial process is beastly and destructive like hunting — it can maim or kill; there is nothing creative about it.

At another point Flory acts according to the public-school spirit and wins Elizabeth's admiration. There is a native uprising brought on by U Po Kyin's machinations and more immediately by Ellis's brutal assault on a Burmese schoolboy. The natives besiege the club where all the British have barred themselves. The surging crowd demands that Ellis be handed over to them for they do not have any faith in British justice. In this hopeless situation, Flory becomes the hero of the moment. Risking his life, he manages to reach the police station and bring sepoys to the rescue of his countrymen. What is more significant is that Flory even assumes the command of the sepoys as their English officer is away. Finally the Burmans are dispersed, and he now believes that he will be able to win Elizabeth. However, Flory's assumption of the role of a *sahib* is fruitless. At a Sunday morning service, Flory's Burmese ex-mistress, acting as part of U Po Kyin's intrigue, denounces him openly. There is no forgiveness from Elizabeth for the hypocritical code of the *sahibs* demands that one's prestige must never be lost in public. Flory commits suicide; both the Raj and the spirit of Burma have destroyed him; suicide is the only appropriate course of action left for him.

CONCLUSION: THE RAJ IS NOT SO BAD AFTER ALL

Orwell rejects the Raj along with all its attendant myths, showing with great realism the immorality, injustice, and hypocrisy of the entire colonial system – he particularly points out that the economic exploitation of other people is the real motive behind imperialism though it is often concealed behind pious theories such as the white man's burden. However, despite such a clear understanding of the colonial process, Orwell at times exhibits feelings and ideas that tend to modify his avowed position on the Raj. He seems to have a Kiplingesque side to his personality which complicates the issue to a certain extent.

Orwell has a great deal in common with Kipling. A similar background, public school education, extended exposure to life in the Indian Empire, produced certain similarities in their attitudes and values though they look so different on the surface. In this regard Orwell's brilliant defence of Kipling, his nostalgia for a romantic concept of Empire, his love for Britain's past and a dread of the future should be noted. Moreover, during his service with the Imperial Indian Police, Orwell proved to be quite an efficient officer and did not appear to have any liberal tendencies. It is true that he did develop a guilt complex later on, but the fact remains that he never seriously espoused the cause of Burmese or Indian independence – he never fought against imperialists the way he did against fascists and communists. Besides, he could never come to love the natives as, for example, Kipling did. In *Burmese Days*, which is his most extended exposure of the Raj, one can see similar attitudes. Here the Raj is not the only evil force at work; Burma is an equally and perhaps more sinister and malignant power – she is the familiar dark force one meets in Kipling's or Forster's Indian works. Both the Raj and Burma destroy Flory, the central character of the novel. And Flory, though he seems to express Orwell's views on the Raj, is not altogether an admirable character – he is presented as a sick man; so one begins to wonder whether one should have complete faith in him or not. Moreover, he does assume the role of a *sahib* in the end when he quells a riot; it is only in that scene that he rises to some heroic proportion, however short-lived his heroism may be. Besides, almost all the Burmese in the novel are cast in a bad light. The one Asian who is presented as a good man worthy of our sympathy is the Indian Dr Veraswami who sickens Flory with his praises for the Raj; this of course is ironical, but still Veraswami manages to make a case for the continuation of the Raj. Veraswami talks about the practical advantages of the Raj – introduction of Western technology, modern medicine and means of communication, education and administration – this view is shared by Orwell. Writing of Kipling's vision of Empire, he says:

> The nineteenth-century Anglo-Indians, to name the least sympathetic of his idols, were at any rate people who did things. It may be that all they did was evil, but they changed the face of the earth (it is instructive to look at a map of Asia and compare the railway systems of India with that of the surrounding countries), whereas they could have achieved nothing, could not have maintained themselves in power for a single week, if the normal Anglo-Indian outlook had been that of, say, E. M. Forster.
>
> (II, 219)

Another fact that may be underlined is that while he was aware of the immorality of the Raj, in his later writings he tended to tone down his criticism of the Empire for he thought that as compared to other tyrannies, it was relatively mild.[22] In his essay 'Reflections on Gandhi' (1949), Orwell writes:

It is difficult to see how Gandhi's methods could be applied in a country where opponents of the regime disappear in the middle of the night and are never heard of again. Without a free press and the right of assembly, it is impossible not merely to appeal to outside opinion, but to bring a mass movement into being, or even to make your own intentions known to your adversary. Is there a Gandhi in Russia at this moment?

(IV, 529)

He wanted to be objective and expected the Indians to be so in their attack on the Raj. Thus in a letter to an Indian published in *Tribune* on 19 March 1943, Orwell states:

We are all nearer to the blimp than we are to the Indian peasant, but don't expect people to like being told so. Opinions sentimentally held are liable to be suddenly reversed. I know more than one intellectual who has started out with a burning zeal to 'free India' and ended up by feeling that there is a lot to be said for General Dyer.[23]

E. M. Forster sums up Orwell's position on the Raj succinctly:

British imperialism, bad as he found it in Burma, is better than the newer imperialisms that are ousting it. All nations are odious but some are less than others, and by this stony, unlovely path he reaches patriotism.[24]

Moreover, the very fact that in his later career he focused his attention on issues other than the Raj indicates that he did not really consider imperialism as that dangerous a problem. I am not suggesting that he wanted the Raj to go on for ever, but certainly his views, taken as a whole, show a remarkable tolerance and even admiration for the Raj. He is not as big an enemy of the Raj as he is generally supposed to be. In fact he is pretty close to Kipling in many ways.

5 John Masters

As an artist, John Masters does not rank with Kipling or Forster though he comes close to them in evoking the sights, smells, and sounds of India. He is seen more or less as a popular soldier-turned-writer of romantic adventure tales in the old tradition. However, I think that there is much more to Masters than a mere narrator of exciting stories. His heroes, for instance, are more complex than they appear to be; they go through doubts and fears, they change and develop, and their essential quest is often as much for identity or relationships as the *dushman* (enemy). And what makes him more important, at least from a historical point of view, is that as a literary chronicler of British India he brings the narrative to the end of the Raj.

Masters has sought, in his novels, to recount some aspects of the complex history of the Raj in India from the beginning to the end through the fortunes of one family, the Savages, which gives a sense of continuity to the whole period. The series deals with the India of the seventeenth century (*Coromandel!*), the time (early nineteenth century) of the murderous thugs (*The Deceivers*), the Mutiny of 1857 (*Nightrunners of Bengal*), the tense situation with Russia in the 1880s (*The Lotus and the Wind*), and the period just before independence in 1947 (*Bhowani Junction*). Moreover, his non-fiction, particularly his autobiographical work, is also helpful in understanding British India at the end of the Raj.

Masters's account of India, even if one may not agree with his point of view, is quite authentic. It is an India with which he and his family have had a long association that goes back five generations at least, being connected mostly with the police or army. Masters, whose father was a captain in the 16th Rajputs, was born in Calcutta in 1914. And after graduation from Sandhurst in 1934, he too joined the Indian Army and saw action on many fronts, particularly during the Second World War. On the independence of India and Pakistan in 1947, Masters resigned from the Indian Army and settled down in the United States where he now lives and writes.

It is indeed a curious transformation from a professional British soldier to a professional American writer. His first novel, *Nightrunners of Bengal*, appeared in 1951 and was received well. Since then he has published about sixteen novels as well as other non-fictional work. Of all these writings, his two volumes of autobiography, *Bugles and a Tiger* (1955) and *The Road Past Mandalay* (1961), and two novels, *Nightrunners of Bengal* (1951) and *Bhowani Junction* (1954), are most pertinent to this study; hence they will be the focus of my attention.

SOMETHING OF MYSELF: *BUGLES AND A TIGER* AND *THE ROAD PAST MANDALAY*

I have used the title of Kipling's reticent autobiography *Something of Myself* as part of the above heading for I feel that Masters has learnt a great deal from the old master. Masters was so immersed in Kipling that he often knew a place long before he actually reached there. For example, on his transfer to the Small Arms School at Pachmarhi, in the Central Provinces, he looks up at a map and notices the name 'Seeone Hills', and at once he remembers:

> This was the country of the *Jungle Books*. Kipling's genius for transmitting atmosphere had been here, and that was why I already half knew the place. Later, when I first went into the Himalayas, I was to recognize that I had travelled in them too, with Kim. It was in the pages of *Kim*, the best book that has ever been written on India, that I had felt the tang of the air and heard the silence, and seen 'the appalling sweep and dispersal of the cloud shadows after rain.'[1]

Similarly, Kipling's words run in his mind as his platoon climbs a jagged hillside during a campaign in Waziristan:

> The eagles is screamin' around us, the river's a-moanin' below,
> We're clear o' the pine an' the oak-scrub, we're out
>   on the rocks an' the snow,
> An' the wind is as thin as a whip-lash what carries
>   away to the plains
> The rattle an' stamp of the lead mules, the jinglety-jink
>   o' the chains — 'Tss! 'Tss!
>
>   (BT, 211)

Kipling and Masters are linked together by their deep interest in India. Like Kipling he also was angry at the British ignorance of India — 'I found myself resenting England's total unawareness of this country' (BT, 81). He wanted to understand both India and its peoples in an objective, realistic way:

> I did not like hearing Indians spoken of as 'niggers', 'wogs', 'Hindoos', or even 'black-bellied bastards' — the standard terms of the British soldier and often of the British Service Officer. . . . On the other hand, I had never had the attitude of the average civilian tourist, so I did not think of India as quaint, picturesque, exploited, inscrutable, or other-worldly. I thought India was ugly, beautiful, smelly, predictable, and as material as the West. It was inhabited not by yogis and saints, but by people — knaves, giants, dwarfs, and plain people — of various shades of brown.
>
> (BT, 81)

And in this approach to India, he makes a great deal of protestation about his love for the country, something which he believes he shares with Kipling:

> But his [Kipling's] descriptions — the turn of a phrase that caught exactly some intonation I had just heard, some sight and smell of the Indian road I had just traveled, some breath from the mountains beyond my window — what of these? These proved that he did love India. No one could write like that except from love.
>
> (BT, 81)

Towards the end of *Bugles and a Tiger*, he affirms his love for India [2] and refuses to quit the country: 'To hell with justification. Let someone else worry about that. I was in love with India, and she'd have the hell of a job getting rid of me.' (BT, 302)

The purpose of *Bugles and a Tiger* is to 'tell the story of how a schoolboy became a professional soldier' and in doing so Masters also hopes 'to have given an idea of what India was like in those last twilight days of the Indian Empire' (BT, 6). He begins the story in mid-1930s in Waziristan where he was first stationed on joining the army, and tells in detail about his acceptance by the 4th Gurkhas — something that he had always wanted. It was there that his life-long sympathy and love for the Gurkhas began.

Bugles and a Tiger focuses on life in the Indian Army. It is filled with action, danger, death, drill parades, mess parties, high living, and boredom, glory, and horror of a way of life now gone for ever. Masters, like Kipling, is able to give us an insight into the life of both the officer and the ordinary soldier. The Tommy was in no enviable position even in the 1930s and 1940s. 'A private's life was no riot in Kipling's day,' Masters notes, 'and it became even less so later.' (BT, 160) There was, for instance, no social life for a private; all he could have was some cheap drink in the bazaar; sand-harlots, riddled with venereal disease; old-fashioned barracks; a cinema a mile away; and, close at hand, boredom, loneliness, and despair.

The officers were better off – they had their clubs and women. The officers' club fulfilled the functions which in a big city are shared between hotels, country clubs, bridge clubs, and other forms of human association.[3] Masters gives a more detailed picture of the *memsahib* in India. She lived her life against a background of scandal centred at Simla or Ranikhet during the summer season. 'The interested watcher,' writes Masters, 'such as, say, Kipling or the present writer – saw strange things.' He elaborates:

> Captain A. comes up to join his wife in Mussoorie for his month's leave. The station forms a wordless conspiracy never to let him know of the existence of Mr. B., a resident official who has, they all know, spent most of his nights and days with Mrs. A. for some weeks past, and will resume this practice as soon as Captain A. has returned to Sweattypore. . . . Women who are thought to be, and in fact are, kind ladies and good mothers, engage in pointed and bitter underground wars, where victory is not measured by beauty, clothes, wit, or intelligence, but by ability to annex the most desirable man and hold on to him in the face of all competition.
>
> (BT, 138–9)

The *memsahib* had her scores of servants to tend to every chore,[4] and thus she had nothing much to do except indulge in socialising, scandal-mongering, or internal feuds. However, life in India was not a bed of roses even for a *memsahib*. Details of material comfort varied and then there was always the danger of disease: rabies, typhoid, smallpox and cholera rampant; snakes, mosquitoes, and scorpions abundant; and sunstroke common. Summing up, Masters says: 'seldom in history have women been subjected at one and the same time to so many discomforts, so much monotony, and so many temptations.' (BT, 149)

Towards the end of the book, Masters briefly turns his attention to Indian political issues. In 1938, on his return to Bombay from Europe, he met some 'nationalists' through an Anglo-Indian friend; they told him clearly that they wanted the British to leave India as soon as the Indians were ready for the responsibility, and Masters tended to agree with them:

> Certainly they wanted us to go, and I at once saw the justice of this. . . . They were for India, with no buts or maybes, yet they recognized that India's interests were often the same as England's . . . They thought, on the whole, that the quickest and best way of getting independence for India was to prove that Indians would be capable of handling it when it came. This attitude was a notable contrast to that of most Indian politicians, particularly of the Congress party, who seemed set on proving only that they could never be trusted with anything more delicately adjusted than a crowbar.
>
> (BT, 264)

It is obvious that the 'nationalists' he meets are no true nationalists — they are Anglo-Indians who never wanted England to quit India. His antipathy for the Congress and its demand for total freedom for India is quite apparent. Later, standing beside the Indus, he looks across India and bursts out with great emotion:

> In whatever spirit the tilling, the land was irrigated with English blood. We were none of us quite strangers, nor ever would be. Nor were we at home, as in our own homes. If we loved and served, we were the heralds of some truer service yet to come in the world, running our blind courses in the darkness of our time and throwing a little light in a few places. We were intruders, yet there are illogical necessities in history, which India understands, because India sees no truth in logic. We were imperialists, and perhaps it was for empire that my Uncle Dandy died at Festubert and the Sikhs died across his feet; but the word their bodies formed as they lay in the pattern of death was not 'lead' or 'obey', but 'give'.
>
> (BT, 300–1)

This statement confirms Masters's faith in the imperial idea and its mystique: it was a God-given duty for the Anglo-Saxons to rule and serve; it was a kind of trust which had been passed on to them at this moment in history; it was their mission to spread light in dark places; imperialism was nothing but an ideal of service and sacrifice. It is rather hard to reconcile such a blind faith in the imperial idea with Masters's claim of being free of any race-consciousness. And soon he simply forgets all about finding a justification for the British hold on India; the British are here by rights of possession:

> To hell with justification. Let someone else worry about that. I was in love with India, and she'd have the hell of a job getting rid of me. I was the adjutant of the 2nd Battalion, 4th Prince of Wales's Own Gurkha Rifles, and I had been formed by my blood, my country, my profession, my regiment, and India.
>
> (BT, 302–3)

The Road Past Mandalay carries the narrative through to the end of the Second World War, telling the story of 'how a professional officer of the old Indian Army reached some sort of maturity both as a soldier and a man'.[5] Much of this story is taken up by an account of Masters's exploits in the Middle East in 1941 and later on the Burmese front in 1944–5. It is a highly vivid description of the pain, suffering and danger of war, and despite Masters's denial, it reads like an authentic battle diary. It is thus quite different from the earlier volume, *Bugles and a Tiger*. *Bugles*, besides giving a sketch of Masters's life, depicts the India of the times. *The Road Past Mandalay* has no such overt aims; its focus is on 'the story of one man's life' (RM, viii).

However, occasionally in *The Road Past Mandalay* one gets some glimpses into Masters's mind and heart that are relevant to this study. The first thing that emerges from this book is Masters's deep attachment to India and the soldiers, particularly Gurkhas.[6] Secondly, one notices that the war and of course the years mellow him. In 1939, while he was a young adjutant, he was shocked at the posting of an Indian as medical officer to his battalion. A few years later the levelling hand of death and war makes him see all fighting men as brothers:

> No one who saw the 14th Army in action, above all, no one who saw its dead on the field of battle, the black and the white and the brown and the yellow on the rich soil of Burma, can ever doubt

that there is a brotherhood of man; or fail to cry, 'What *is* Man, that
he can give so much for war, so little for peace?'

(RM, 154–5)

Another lesson that he now learns is to value personal relationships
such as with Barbara whom he married or his Gurkha orderly Daljit.
At a crucial moment in his life, he becomes aware of the supreme
importance of personal relationships:

> But supposing I learned that to become a general I must give up
> service with Gurkhas. I would not do it, because the wonder of
> living lay not in the abstractions of command, as such, but in a
> direct personal relationship with men like Daljit.

(RM, 116)

Despite these noble sentiments, it is disappointing to note that
Masters's stand on the Raj does not change much. As a soldier he tried
to keep politics out of his mind — at best it was an attitude of
indifference: 'When the time came, someone would tell us to go
home; meanwhile we had a job to do.' (RM, 18) At places, however,
he records how the Congress's 'Quit India' campaign never reached
the countryside:

> In the course of a thousand miles walked through the country
> between Jhansi and Jubbulpore I questioned several score villagers
> in different places as to what they knew about the political situation
> in India, and the war. Most had heard of the war. Two had heard of
> the Indian National Congress and three of Gandhi.

(RM, 134)

Masters's emphasis is on the British work in India rather than its
drawbacks; on the bond between the British and the Indians, though
he knows that it was never a relationship of equality but that does not
matter:

> Certainly we had been masters, and imperialists, but we had not
> been afraid to die with these men and we had always loved them
> and their country, usually with intense, blind passion which could
> ignore all theoretical considerations of right and wrong.

(RM, 307)

This kind of belief in a benevolent master-servant relationship sounds awfully old-fashioned in mid-twentieth century, but that is how Masters feels and thinks that this feudalistic 'love and understanding' made the nationalists' argument redundant. He is not ashamed to be an imperialist, for the Raj, in his view, has done wonders to this land; the greatest wonder of all is that it turned the heterogeneous country called India into a unity that it never was:

> When my great-great-grandfather first went to India there had been as many nations; now there was one — India; and he and I and a few thousand others, over two and a half centuries, sometimes with intent, sometimes unwittingly, sometimes in miraculous sympathy, sometimes in brutal folly, had made it. Whether we ought to have gone to India in the first place is a moral problem of meaning not only to England, because it is quite certain that if we had not taken over, France or Russia would have. Nor can we know what they would have made of the ramshackle subcontinent they would have found. I only know that I saw, beside the road outside Pyawbwe, what *we* had made.
>
> (RM, 308)

This statement is perhaps historically correct, but I do not see how one can get away from facing the very serious moral issues involved in imperialism on the basis of welding the country together.

THE MUTINY: *NIGHTRUNNERS OF BENGAL*

The year 1857 stands as a landmark in the history of India for it saw the first national struggle for liberation which almost shook the foundations of the Company Bahadur's Raj. More has been written about this event than any other in the long years of British occupation of India. Most British writers dismiss it as a mere revolt of disgruntled elements in the army or at best a half-hearted attempt on the part of the fast-fading Indian aristocracy to regain its lost power; they refer to it as the Sepoy Mutiny rather than a true war of independence and see it as another episode of British heroism, another proof of the superiority of the imperial race.

The mutiny was, however, not just a military rebellion nor a hysterical reaction of the old aristocracy threatened with extinction.[7] It was above all a spontaneous expression of the grievances of the

Indian masses against a tyrannical, alien misrule.[8] The Indians only had to look around them to see the British interfering at every level of life; they feared and resented this interference that threatened their identity, culture, and religion. It was against this background of widespread discontent that a mass uprising started against the *ferangi* (the British), a rising in which Muslim and Hindu united.

The rebellion, though finally crushed, was a bloody and brutal affair. There were atrocities on both sides. Sepoys killed the beleaguered British, including women and children, in the earlier days of the Mutiny though on a much smaller scale than the British public was led to believe. And there were many Indians who protected the British despite grave danger to themselves. Nevertheless, the British avenged themselves with a savagery seldom witnessed. While rebel sepoys were blown to death from the mouth of the cannon, civilians were hanged on a mass scale. There was hardly a tree without a corpse hanging on its branches; volunteer hanging parties went out into the districts, and amateur executioners found delight in finishing the Indians off 'in an artistic manner' such as the figure of eight – these executions were known as 'Colonel Neill's hangings'.

The Mutiny opened a gulf of hatred and distrust between the British and the Indians which could not be bridged completely later on. It also saw the demise of the East India Company; the transfer of India to the Crown; and the beginning of a process which culminated in the independence of the sub-continent in 1947.

In *Nightrunners of Bengal*, Masters has captured some of the pain, horror, and violence of the turbulent days of the Mutiny as well as its causes and effects. In his foreword, he writes:

> England – Victoria's pompous, stolid Christian England – sprang up in an ecstasy of outrage, to answer murder with mass murder, and hate with a demoniacal fury of hate. Twelve centuries of English history show nothing remotely like it. This was at once the noon of courage and the midnight of barbarism.[9]

As for the cause, Masters, in a Forster-like manner, finds it in the indifference of the British towards Indians; in their refusal to establish personal relationships with the natives: 'they [the British] were like men in an upstairs room, secure, cut off. . . . So the house cracked. The world cracked.' (NB, viii)

Masters's story is set in the imaginary town of Bhowani,[10] a small military station on the outskirts of the state of Kishanpur of which it originally formed a part. We are given a fairly credible account of the privileged life of the 'Anglo-Indians' of the time, the emphasis being on the division between the British and the natives. The world of the *sahibs*, particularly that of the *memsahib*, has no place for the Indian except in the role of a servant. Joanna, the wife of Captain Rodney Savage — the protagonist of the novel — is a typical *memsahib*. Despite six years in India, she hardly knows twenty words of Hindustani; she insists on calling her servants blacks; her interest lies in balls, fancy dresses and liaisons; she reminds one of Mrs Hauksbee, the socialite of Kipling's Simla.

Caroline Langford, a recent visitor to India, is set up as a contrast to Joanna and other Englishwomen in Bhowani. She is interested in knowing India and Indians; she has already spent six months alone in the state of Kishanpur; and while in Bhowani she does not hesitate to go to the bazaar all by herself. In some ways she is like Forster's Adela Quested though the differences are also obvious; Adela rejects imperialism, but Caroline is a firm believer in the Raj and the imperial idea.

As others dance at the club in the New Year of 1857, Caroline subjects Rodney to a barrage of penetrating questions, particularly on the issue of the gulf between the British and the Indians. Rodney admits that there is no real social contact between the two sides; that in order to feel India in the way she wants, one must become Indian and 'as a race we don't do it — we can't' (NB, 18); and that perhaps it is best to keep things the way they are. With complacency he adds that as far as he is concerned, he knows his sepoys well. Finally, their conversation changes to the possibility of a rebellion by the Indians. 'Doesn't he [the Indian] want to be his own master?' asks Caroline. And Rodney gives the traditional reply:

> Perhaps, if it were possible. But first he wants peace and protection — which means power — and we're giving them to him . . . sometimes I feel ashamed. Take this very Bhowani Territory. It used to be part of Kishanpur State, as I expect you heard when you were there. We took it on a forced lease — in perpetuity — but we really have no right here. Yet now the peasants and the lower castes generally would do anything rather than revert to Kishanpur rule.
>
> (NB, 20)

Rodney's argument for the Raj is based on the practical benefits of British rule rather than its moral or legal right.

The scene then shifts to another India – the princely India – as Rodney is despatched to restore law and order in the neighbouring Kishanpur state where the Rajah has been assassinated. What follows is a thrilling tale of palace intrigues, adventure, and sex in a highly exotic setting. Here we meet another major character of the novel – Sumitra, the Rani of Kishanpur and a leader of the Mutiny, who seems to have been modelled on the famous Rani of Jhansi.[11] She is presented as a courageous, patriotic, charming young woman with the morals of a harlot. Where she cannot buy with money, she offers herself in order to attain her goals. She takes a fancy to Rodney and wants him to command her forces. However, our hero resists all these temptations – he is so devoted to his duty. Sumitra too is following her duty, the nationalist's duty of ousting the foreigners from the land: 'I killed my husband for India; I pretended to be a whore for India; I lied, for India. I am Indian first and woman afterward' (NB, 231), she declares openly.

Soon after Rodney's return to Bhowani, the Mutiny breaks out; and Rodney, as he stands in the blood-bath around him, is overcome with shame at English failure in India – 'All that he had failed. The English in India had failed England; the Bengal Army had failed these men; they, who were a part of him, had failed themselves.' (NB, 195) Rodney along with his little son is able to escape though Joanna is killed. Guided by Peroo, the Indian carpenter of his regiment, Rodney joins Caroline and seeks refuge in Kishanpur. However, he soon becomes suspicious of the Rani's intentions towards the British, and flees from her palace. Now he is headed towards Gondwara, a British garrison station.

Much of the story is taken by the description of Rodney's escape as he travels through the countryside and jungle trails, brushing closely with death. This narrative also brings into focus the hospitality and humanity of Indian villagers who offer them food and shelter though they themselves are suffering from the ravages of war and disease. Their sacrifice is best illustrated in the way the priest of Chalisgaon saves the life of Caroline with his last supply of opium, the only remedy known at the time against cholera, although he or his family could have fallen sick and no opium was available for miles around. This incident makes Rodney aware of the need of love on the part of the English if they really wanted to stay in the country. Rodney is ready to love Indians, but he is not prepared to hand them back their country for he is convinced that the Indians cannot handle the job:

> The Company is not going to lose India . . . and if it did, do you
> think Indians are fit to rule themselves, or protect themselves, yet?
> There'd be a year of anarchy, civil wars between rajahs mad for
> power. I know now why the Rani wanted me to command her
> army. And who would suffer in all that but the ordinary people of
> India? And afterward – Russia!
>
> (NB, 285)

Finally Rodney reaches Gondwara and sees signs of British
brutality all over. Here he reports to General Hector for duty and is
instrumental in identifying the rebellious sepoys. Shortly afterwards,
the British forces march toward Kishanpur and invade the state. The
Rani, who had been an active leader of the Mutiny, is intercepted by
Rodney as she tries to flee the area. However, she refuses to surrender
and jumps to her death in a nearby river with these last words: 'But
the rebellion will go on, until I and those who will follow me are
wiped out.' (NB, 329)

TOWARDS FREEDOM: *BHOWANI JUNCTION*

The setting of *Bhowani Junction* (1954) remains the same as that of
Nightrunners of Bengal, but the time has changed. Instead of 1857, it is
now 1946 – another period of crisis on the eve of independence to
which the bloody events of the Mutiny had inevitably led. By the late
thirties the British were more or less reconciled to the idea of leaving
the country at some point. The idea was not a voluntary one; it had
been painfully forced upon them through half a century of nationalist
agitation, massive unrest, sporadic outbreaks of rebellion, and two
world wars which exhausted the British will and ability to hold the
colonies. The Second World War helped to hasten the process of
independence. By June 1942 the Japanese had swept forward to the
eastern front of India; they, along with the Germans, were encourag-
ing Indians to armed uprising against the British through sponsoring
an Indian National Army called 'Azad Hind Fauj' under Subhas
Chandra Bose (1897– 1945); so communist and fascist threats were
very real. Taking advantage of the situation, Gandhi led the Congress
in a demand to the British to quit India that was followed by a mass
non-violent, civil disobedience that paralysed the country. In 1940

the Muslim League had put forward the two nation theory and made a demand for Pakistan, a separate homeland for Muslims, which complicated matters. And there were large scale communal riots threatening to engulf the country in a civil war. The failing power of the British to enforce control was particularly emphasised by the 1946 mutiny of some units of the Indian Navy in Bombay and Karachi. The naval mutiny lasted only five days, but it raised fears of another 1857. The British were no longer masters of the situation, and were ready to leave as soon as a settlement acceptable to the people of India was found.

Bhowani Junction gives us a feel of this atmosphere of tension and uncertainty at the end of the Raj. However, the main focus of the novel is something else; its real theme is the plight of the Anglo-Indians on the eve of independence. The rising tide of Indian nationalism caught the Anglo-Indian community rather unprepared. Numerically insignificant, they presented a particularly tragic problem. Midway between two cultural worlds, under the peculiar conditions of their origin and socio-cultural development, they could never really get to know the West to which they aspired to belong, nor did they have any emotional ties with India where they really belonged. The sudden decision of the British to withdraw from the country and the rapid transformation of the cultural scene in the land posed very serious problems for the community, involving questions of identity and survival among people whom they had always hated — more than the British, the Anglo-Indians made it a point to call Indians 'wogs' or 'niggers'.[12] They felt angry, helpless, and betrayed.[13] In *Bhowani Junction*, in which the narrative is divided between three protagonists, a story of communist sabotage, terrorism, and political agitation in the exciting days of the Quit India Movement serves as a background for a search for identity on the part of Anglo-Indians in a rapidly changing India.

Patrick Taylor, the district traffic superintendent at Bhowani Junction, is a typical Anglo-Indian who refuses to see the writing on the wall. Proud of his old school tie from St Thomas's at Gondwara — an Anglo-Indian school in danger of being closed down and symbolic of the fate of the entire community — he remains steadfast in his hatred of the Indians whom he continues to call wogs. He gets the shock of his life when he finds that Victoria, his girl-friend, no longer feels the same way about Indians.

Victoria Jones, an Anglo-Indian railway girl, is the attractive, brown-eyed, dark-haired heroine of the story. She has been away from Bhowani as an officer with the Women's Auxiliary Corps for four years and has acquired a different, more mature perspective. She tells Patrick that things are changing fast and that they should not keep their eyes closed:

> I've been four years among only Englishmen and Indians. Do you realize that they hardly know there *is* such a thing as an Anglo-Indian community? Once I heard an old English colonel talking to an Indian — he was a young fellow, a financial adviser. The colonel said, 'What are you going to do about the Anglo-Indians when we leave?' 'We're not going to do anything, Colonel,' the Indian said. 'Their fate is in their own hands. They've just got to look around and see where they are and who they are — after you've gone.'[14]

But Patrick and other Anglo-Indians at Bhowani refuse to listen to her; they do not think that the English can ever leave them. And if they do, Patrick declares that he will go with them: 'My God, if they leave, I will go Home with them.' (BJ, 21) Victoria screams back, 'Home! Where is your home, man? England? . . . I am only asking you to think.' (BJ, 21) And Patrick realises the peculiar dilemma of the entire community: '. . . we *couldn't* go Home. We couldn't become English, because we were half Indian. We couldn't become Indians, because we were half English.' (BJ, 21)

In the meantime, Bhowani is swept by the storm of political agitation and violence. The supposedly non-violent civil disobedience movement launched by the Congress in the wake of its Quit India demand was not always without violence for it was often infiltrated by extremists such as communists or fascists. K. P. Roy is presented as a representative of these extremist elements who are using the Congress for their own ends. The liberal, genuine Congress *wallahs* are portrayed by the local Congress boss Surabhai who is preoccupied with democratic ideals and human rights. Surabhai is treated with sympathy by Masters. However, Masters also indicates the ineffectiveness of liberal politicians like Surabhai in either protecting people from the manipulations of extremists like K. P. Roy or in their failure in translating their ideals into reality. Each time Surabhai arranges a demonstration or strike, something goes wrong; in the end he himself falls a victim to the forces of terrorism that he unwittingly helps unleash. Moreover, the sorry figure that Surabhai cuts all the time is another comment on Masters's point of view about the Congress and the independence movement in general.

Victoria, who is deeply affected by the course of events, gradually attempts to identify herself with India. This drift towards India is strengthened by the clumsiness of Patrick as well as the unfeeling attitude of the British. Colonel Savage, her boss, never misses a chance to put her in her place while the other British officer, Macaulay, takes her for a tart and tries to rape her. She kills Macaulay and at a time when she does not know where to turn for help, Patrick's young Sikh assistant, Ranjit Singh Kasel, comes to her rescue. She now attaches herself to Ranjit.

Victoria had been searching for her roots for a long time; now she thinks that she has found where she should belong. Much to the horror of her family, she throws out her Western clothes and puts on a *sari*. She becomes engaged to Ranjit and prepares to adopt the Sikh religion in order to marry him. However, she is always conscious of some distance between her and Ranjit despite her devotion to him. During the elaborate ceremony of her initiation into the Sikh fold, she realises that she does not really love Ranjit and that a change of religion cannot alter her Anglo-Indian identity. She thus runs out of the *gurdwara* (Sikh temple) and that is the end of her search for her Indian roots.

Her father receives Victoria with tears of joy hoping that she will someday marry a real Englishman such as Colonel Rodney Savage. She does capture Rodney; not as a wife, but as a mistress, for being an Anglo-Indian she is not good enough to be his wife. In the end, Victoria goes back to her own people, to Patrick Taylor, whom she finally marries. As Rodney reflects, that was the only course left open to her:

> Patrick was a part of that life. He had become petty, helpless, and hopeless. She'd tried becoming an Indian – but she wasn't an Indian. She'd tried becoming English – but she wasn't English.
>
> (BJ, 372)

Patrick too changes and develops in the end. He realises that the Indians are not going to settle old scores after independence, and he accepts a managerial position in a big cement factory at Cholaghat. After all there will be a place for them in independent India. In this painful acceptance of the new circumstances, both Victoria and Patrick typify the agony of the entire Anglo-Indian community at the end of the Raj.

CONCLUSION: WE ARE HERE TO STAY

John Masters knows his India inside out; he was born there, spent his youth there as a professional soldier, loved and matured there, and was able to see many things which are not experienced by a visitor. He naturally loves India, which forms the central theme of many of his novels. In this respect, he is closer to Kipling than Forster, for the latter had only a temporary contact with the sub-continent. His admiration of the soldier, Indian or British; his sense of local colour, and his belief in duty and action, further link him with Kipling.

However, there are some important differences as well. First of all, he lacks the artistic or philosophic depth of Kipling or Forster; his approach to India is simplistic. Secondly, and this is perhaps an important point, Masters started writing long after the independence of India and Pakistan; consequently, he could not speak about the viability of the imperial idea in his fiction when its breakdown was a *fait accompli* even though he continued to believe in it. It is therefore small wonder that he concentrates on the past glorious days of the Raj; *Bhowani Junction* is the only novel that is set at the time of the break-up of the British rule in India. His autobiographical work is therefore a more trusty guide to his reaction to the Raj.

The two volumes of his autobiography, *Bugles and a Tiger* and *The Road Past Mandalay*, give us some insight into his mind and heart. As a young officer in the Indian Army, he never questioned the Raj or its wars; in fact he took the Raj for granted. Surely, he came to love his Gurkhas and learnt to value personal relationships, but it never occurred to him that he had no right to rule the land. He talks a great deal about his liberalism while he accuses Kipling of racial prejudice, but he forgets that Kipling was writing in the heyday of British imperialism and for his time he shows a progressive attitude in holding a philosophic concept of the Empire; moreover, Kipling's racism is more apparent than real.

Masters is at pains to justify the presence of the British in India on the basis of their work — law and order; building of roads, railways, and communications; trade and industry; and health and education. He cites all the historical facts — the rooting out of *thuggee*, abolition of *suttee*, political reforms and so on. But often he seems to imply that Indians are not capable of ruling themselves; that the British, right or wrong, have conquered the land; and therefore they are not going to leave it unless they are made to. On occasion, he also indicates his conviction in the providential destiny of the British to rule and serve the rest of mankind. The upholding of such beliefs in the 1880s can be understood, but they sound bizarre in the 1950s.

In his fiction, Masters adopts a historical and more objective attitude towards the Empire, mainly because he is writing after the independence of the sub-continent. Here he traces the history of the Raj through the adventures of the Savages – Captain Rodney Savage may in fact be taken as his mask or persona though at times he appears to be more flexible and modern than Masters.

In *Nightrunners of Bengal*, for instance, not the slightest hint of contempt is shown for the Rani of Kishanpur, a major leader of the Mutiny. She is presented as an intelligent, capable, patriotic, person who is defeated not because her cause is unworthy or that she is lacking in courage; she loses because circumstances are against her, the forces of history are moving India in a direction away from the feudal order. Masters' objectivity is further evident from his horror of the cruelty of his compatriots that was shown during the suppression of the Mutiny. Conversely, he emphasises the humanity of many Indians who protected the British in times of trouble despite threats to their own lives. Masters also criticises the British for their lack of personal contact with the natives; this is seen as a prime cause of the discontent against the Raj. Here Masters comes close to Forster's diagnosis of the break-up of the Raj: undeveloped heart, lack of personal contact and general good will.

In *Bhowani Junction* Masters even grudgingly accepts the fact of impending independence though he is not sure whether the Congress can run the country efficiently; the Congress will at least need British-trained and Westernised native administrators like Govindaswami if India is to be saved from total chaos. The British, he implies, are big enough to get reconciled to the realities of the situation; this is exemplified by the way Colonel Savage, whose ancestors suppressed the Mutiny in 1857, is playing a crucial role in keeping law and order so that peaceful transfer of power may be effected.

Thus there remains a slight gap between his fiction and non-fiction as far as Masters' attitude towards the imperial idea is concerned. This discrepancy, as suggested earlier, is caused by the fact that he started writing after the independence of the sub-continent; he simply could not ignore a historical fact. However, acceptance of the fact of independence in his fiction does not necessarily imply his rejection of the imperial idea in which, as indicated by his non-fiction, he seems to firmly believe. By accepting the changing realities of the Indo-Pakistani political situation, Masters is only showing his pragmatism or historical sense rather than a real change of heart. As compared to Forster or even Kipling, he remains a conservative, a supporter of the imperial idea.

6 Epilogue

With the growth of nationalism and the ebbing of imperialism at the turn of the century, the literature of the Raj, a genre established by Kipling, underwent a corresponding change. One thing which is immediately obvious is that in the post-1914 period it became increasingly difficult for a writer working within the imperial context to share Kipling's confidence and faith in the Raj and the imperial idea without serious doubts and fears. The degree of these doubts and fears about the future and validity of the Raj of course varies with individual writers. Nevertheless the era of confidence was gone for ever; it was now replaced by an era of doubt and melancholy.

However, what is interesting to note is that the English literary reaction to the changing political and historical realities of the sub-continent does not express itself in a simple pro- or anti-Raj position as literary historians tend to believe. The large majority of these writers, like the then majority of the British public, display mixed feelings; they seem to be aware of the justice of the nationalists' case and they recognise the moral confusion involved in the colonial process, and yet they cannot help admiring the Raj. What is curious is that most of these writers fail to realise that the psychology of the Raj was really based on a lie; to them all the romantic myths about the Raj popularised by Kipling appear very appealing. The shadow of Kipling looms heavily on the entire period right up to the break-up of the Raj in 1947.

This fact is clearly established by the foregoing analysis of the major post-Kipling writers on the Raj. E. M. Forster, despite his liberal humanism and condemnation of the 'Anglo-Indians', does not espouse the cause of India's freedom; he cherishes a continuing British connection with India though on more equal footing. E. J. Thompson says the same thing in a less artistic manner and he devotes half his energies to a vigorous defence of the Raj on the basis of all the benefits it has brought to India. George Orwell too belongs to the camp of the admirers of the Raj though his occasional attack on imperialism may lead one to think otherwise. Orwell's criticism of the Raj is countered by a corresponding hatred of the colonised and a view that the Raj is after all not entirely evil and that it has a redeeming side to it – the Raj comes out with flying colours when compared with fascism or communism, he seems to imply. With John Masters we are back to square one. Although Masters writes in the post-independence period, he is more interested in the glorious past of the Raj when it was not contaminated by any doubts; so he can restate the whole argument for the Raj in Kiplingesque terms. The journey from Forster to Masters brings us back to the old master – Rudyard Kipling.

Notes

CHAPTER I

1. George Lichtheim, *Imperialism* (New York, 1971), p. 5.
2. Ibid., p. 6.
3. For example *pax Romana* embodied these ideas. This conception of a single empire wielding authority over the world did not disappear with the fall of Rome — it survived all the fluctuations of the Holy Roman Empire. And in later ages this dream of a universal empire animated the policies of Peter the Great, Catherine and Napoleon. The idea of a universal empire was not confined to the West alone — witness the Chinese, Byzantine or Arab empires; and political philosophers in many ages — Confucius, Dante, Machiavelli, Vico, Kant — have speculated on the concept.
4. A. P. Thornton, *The Imperial Idea and its Enemies* (London, 1966), p. ix. It may be observed that the imperial idea, though admirable in certain ways, was strongly tinged with a belief in the racial and cultural superiority of the white man. However, at that time this superiority was taken for granted — it was sanctioned by social, anthropological, and even religious attitudes. The upholders of this idea were often not guilty of any hypocrisy — they really believed that they were bringing progress to Asia or Africa by ruling it.
5. The days of the Company's rule (except for Bentinck's viceroyalty) are a nightmarish record of unscrupulous plundering by a joint-stock company. Fabulous fortunes were made in a short time by individuals as well who returned to England as self-styled *nabobs*. Clive himself, who started with nothing, returned home with quarter of a million pounds and an Indian estate. The frequent famines of Bengal, the richest province of India before the takeover by the Company, were a direct result of British looting.
6. James Mill, *History of British India* (London, 1820), V, 416.
7. India was seen by these thinkers as a *tabula rasa* where they could freely experiment with their social or religious theories, which could not be done at home because of the conservatism of British life. The reformers of the early nineteenth century did not assess correctly the problems and institutions of India. See Francis G. Hutchins, *The Illusion of Permanence* (Princeton, 1967).
8. Lord Curzon, Speech in Bombay, 16 November 1905. See George Bennett (ed.), *The Concept of Empire: Burke to Attlee, 1774–1947* (London, 1953), p. 105.
9. Jawaharlal Nehru, *Autobiography* (London, 1936), p. 438.
10. For a full treatment of this subject see Thornton, *The Imperial Idea and its Enemies.*
11. Changes in anthropological thinking introduced by Malinowski radically altered the nineteenth-century image of the so-called 'primitive' people. A primitive society was no longer assigned its appropriate niche in the world order. The modern approach to an alien experience is 'what does it mean to them?' not

'how strange it seems to me'. Hence the whole notion of the 'civilised' and 'non-civilised' societies was demolished. The influence of these new ideas in literature may be seen in the post-1914 novels. D. H. Lawrence, for example, gives considerable significance to the symbolism of colours in Aztec ritual, whereas earlier writers had dismissed face-painting as hideous distortions. See Brian V. Street, *The Savage in Literature* (London, 1975), pp. 1–17.

12. For example, in his study of Anglo-Indian fiction, Bhupal Singh lists sixteen pages containing over a thousand titles of works on India and this covers only the period to the mid-1930s. See his *A Survey of Anglo-Indian Fiction* (London, 1934). For Anglo-Indian fiction from mid-1930s to the present time, see bibliography at the end of this study. *The Book Review Digest*, which lists books according to their locale, may also be helpful.

13. It must be noted here that imperialism is not central to Kipling's vision, and that it is modified by his concern with what he calls 'the Law' as well as his curious love-hate relationship with India. Kipling was not a diehard, jingo imperialist or a mere propagandist of the British Empire, though my catalogue of the stock images of India in his works may lead one to believe so. One has to consider in historical perspective both Kipling's concern with a moral responsibility of the empire-builder and his bitter diatribes against his countrymen, in order to form a proper estimate of his imperial philosophy. See my book *Kipling's 'Law': A Study of his Philosophy of Life* (London, 1975).

For a detailed treatment of British images of India see Allen J. Greenberger, *The British Image of India: A Study in the Literature of Imperialism, 1880–1960* (London, 1969).

14. The nineteenth-century Rousseauistic image of primitive man as a sort of noble savage had something to do with this attitude.

15. *The Writings in Prose and Verse of Rudyard Kipling*, 'Outward Bound Edition', 36 vols (New York, 1897–1937), I, 88. Subsequent references to Kipling's works, unless otherwise indicated, will be to this edition.

16. *The Definitive Edition of Rudyard Kipling's Verse* (London, 1954), p. 323. Hereafter referred to as DE. 'The White Man's Burden' was published in 1899 on the eve of the American occupation of the Philippines, and was intended to remind them of their responsibilities.

17. The question of Kipling's racism must be seen in relation to Darwinian anthropology as well as in the attitude of his contemporaries. Henty or Buchan, for example, are outright racists who do not see any saving grace in the natives. On the other hand, Kipling's approach is not simplistic. Often Kipling recognises native qualities or even native superiority over the English, particularly in matters of religion. His Gunga Din is better than a white man; his Fuzzy Wuzzy are superior to the Tommies; and Kamal's son, though a free-booter, is worthy of our admiration. And then there is the Lama in *Kim* who puts a lie to Kipling's so-called racism. The above-quoted line from 'Recessional' should be read within the context of his philosophy of law (which is a principle of order on both external and internal levels) as well as the deep note of humility which marks the whole poem. Moreover, it may also be kept in mind that Kipling's race-consciousness was a natural result of his stay in India, which is the home of diverse races and creeds.

18. Louis Cornell, *Kipling in India* (London, 1966), p. 3.

19. However, this story is also designed to show that the empire-builder has a moral

responsibility to his subjects and that he would lose his empire if he neglects his duty.

20. For a full discussion of this point see Hutchins. pp. 65–78. Sexual depravity was particularly ascribed to climate though Englishmen were not prepared to concede that Indian residence increased their own sexual appetites. Here colour came to their rescue; the dark races were supposed to have sexual inclinations unknown to Europeans.

21. The pro-Muslim attitude that is dominant in English writings on India was based on a number of other factors. Islam sprang from the Judaeo-Christian tradition; Muslims, like the British, came as conquerors to India; they had a tradition of discipline and action; and they were more or less free from the caste system and social evils of Hindus. These were the major elements which appealed to the British.

22. Hutchins, p. 187.

23. Rudyard Kipling, 'The Council of the Gods', *Pioneer*, 18 February 1888.

24. For example, as soon as the English Collector leaves Tibasu in 'His Chance in Life', the town plunges into chaos: '. . . hearing nothing of the Collector-*Sahib* for some time . . . Hindus and Mohammadans together raised an aimless sort of Donnybrook just to see how far they could go. They looted each other's shops, and paid off private grudges in the regular way.' (I, 88–9)

25. Hutchins, p. 186.

26. In a revealing letter to his friend H. A. Gwynne, Kipling confirmed his belief that the establishment of a national administration in India would result in a complete breakdown of law and order: '. . . there will be *suttee* again, dacoity there is already in full flow. Very few of the political movements and *hartals* are unaccompanied by robbery, house-breaking or murderous assaults . . . I only want to save as many lives as are possible.' (The letter is dated 26 November 1930, and it is part of the Stewart Kipling Collection, Dalhousie University, Halifax, Canada.)

27. This, for example, is one of the main points in 'The Enlightenment of Pagett, M. P.' The story is also an attack on the liberal politicians in England who meddle in Indian affairs without knowing much about India. However, in all fairness, one must concede that Kipling is being realistic in certain ways. At that time (1880s) the Congress was a modest organisation that was not popular with the masses, and it was viewed with suspicion by Muslims and Christians.

28. Kipling's well-known story 'The Head of the District' is a case in point. On Orde's death, a Bengali, Grish Chunder De, is appointed as deputy commissioner of a turbulent district on the North West Frontier. The arrival of the Hindu *babu* is the prelude to big trouble; he is simply rejected as a ruler by the Pathans who for centuries harried and controlled Bengal. For them Grish Chunder, despite his excellent academic record, is a *kala admi* (black man) and a Hindu and hence unfit to govern them. Orde was successful not only because he was an Englishman, but also because he ruled the orientals in an oriental fashion. In other words, Kipling here demolishes the idea of self-government or democracy as unsuited to India.

29. Hutchins, pp. 137–52.

30. The Law, as pointed out earlier, is the central theme in Kipling's works, and it seems to signify a principle of order on both external and internal levels. The imperial idea is seen as a means of spreading the Law though it includes other

elements such as belief in action and ethics. See my book *Kipling's Law*.

31. It must however be noted that Kipling's Roman tales not only point out the parallel between the Raj and the Roman Empire, but also the differences between the two or rather between the Raj and Kipling's concept of empire. The religion of Kipling's empire is not Christianity but Mithraism which is closer to the public-school spirit and his philosophy of action. There is no racial, religious, or social discrimination in this empire. And moreover, Roman imperialism, unlike British, was based on law rather than nationality. National identity and national exclusiveness could fire the British to great exploits, but this was not the basis on which a permanent multi-national Raj could be built. So Kipling is criticising the Raj as much as he praises it. In fact, Kipling's concept of empire cannot be identified with British imperialism alone; it is a much larger concept with a strong moral side to it. Also see Hutchins, *Illusion of Permanence*.

32. Although Orwell was born in India, he wrote about Burma where he served in the Police Department for some time. However, as Burma had been part of the Indian Empire since the 1880s, technically he is within the range of the Raj which is the focus of this study. (It may also be observed that during this time Ceylon was also within the Indian Empire.)

33. Among the few studies which come close to this topic, I should mention Benita Parry's *Delusions and Discoveries: Studies on India in the British Imagination, 1880– 1930* (London, 1972) and Allen J. Greenberger's *The British Image of India: A Study in the Literature of Imperialism, 1880–1960* (London, 1969). My study is however more specifically on the imperial idea and English literary reaction to its failure during the twilight days of the Raj (1914–47) rather than a generalised British image of India.

34. It would have been equally interesting to compare and contrast the attitude of Indian writers with that of the English concerning the imperial idea at the end of the Raj. However, for sundry reasons, including my own limitations, I am confining myself to the English writers only. So this is basically a study of the English writers' response to the break-up of the Indian Empire.

CHAPTER 2

1. E. M. Forster, 'The Challenge of Our Time', *Two Cheers for Democracy* (London: Penguin, 1974), p. 64.

2. For example, Edith C. Batho and Bonamy Dobrée in their book *The Victorians and After* (London, 1950) state: 'In his [Forster's] novels and short stories we find the deepest reaction to things that Kipling stood for. Each has a distinct scale of values. . . . For Mr. Forster, Mr. Kipling's world is the useless outer world, a scene of telegrams and anger, of futile efficiency, of misdirected effort.' (pp. 97– 8) It is interesting to note that even a Kipling enthusiast like Dobrée can be swept away by the force of such generalisations.

3. There are some critics who do see similarities. See H. Marshall McLuhan's article, 'Kipling and Forster', *The Sewanee Review*, 52 (1944), 332–43.

4. The publication of *Maurice* in 1971 complicates the matter slightly. However, this novel was written before *A Passage to India* was first attempted, in 1913–14.

5. E. M. Forster, 'Indian Entries', *Encounter*, 28 (January 1962), 20–7.

6. Masood was a grandson of the famous Muslim leader and educationist Sir Syed Ahmad Khan (1817–98) who in 1875 founded the Muslim Anglo-Oriental

College at Aligarh which later became the Muslim University of Aligarh. This university played a central role in the renaissance of the Muslim community in India. Masood was brought to England for education by Theodore Morrison, a close friend of Sir Syed. Masood studied at Oxford but he was not much of a scholar; he barely managed to get a second class degree in history. Later he studied law in London. Soon after meeting him, Forster was enthralled by Masood's warmth as his earliest diary entry clearly tells: 'Dec. 24. Masood gives up duties for friends – which is civilisation. Though as he remarks "Hence the confusion in Oriental states. To them personal relations come first."' (Quoted by P. N. Furbank, *E. M. Forster: A Life*, 2 vols (London, 1977–8), I, 145. I am greatly indebted to Furbank for fresh information on Masood.)

7. During this first trip to India, Forster saw Masood again in January after visiting Dewas. At this time Masood was a magistrate at Bankipore which is a model for the city of Chandrapore in *A Passage to India*. From here Forster proceeded to Allahabad and on his way, he visited the Buddhist sites of Buddh Gaya and the Barbar Hills, later to be a model for the Marabar caves. On the last leg of his journey, Forster went to Aurangabad (in Deccan), where he stayed with Masood's friend Ahmed Mirza's younger brother Abu Saeed Mirza, a junior magistrate. Saeed showed him around the cave-temples of Ellora, and he is reflected in the character of Dr Aziz to a certain extent. See Furbank, *E. M. Forster: A Life* (London, 1977–8).

8. E. M. Forster, *The Hill of Devi* (London, 1953), p. 10.

9. There is some difference of opinion on this point. While it is true that the novel was partly written during Forster's 1921–2 visit and that he experienced the fast-changing political conditions at first hand, the novel's point of view remains that of 1912 rather than 1924. However, an argument has been made that Forster intends the people in the novel to seem totally unaware of the vast changes that had occurred in India since 1912 in order to intensify the political significance and irony of the novel. See Jeffrey Meyers, *Fiction and the Colonial Experience* (Ipswich, 1973), pp. 36–43. Also see G. K. Das who in his recent study *E. M. Forster's India* (London, 1977) makes an interesting case for the novel's absorption of contemporary political events.

10. Without warning, General Dyer dispersed a prohibited political meeting of ten thousand people in an enclosed garden by firing 1650 rounds, killing over three hundred people and injuring over a thousand. This incident alienated even the pro-British elements of Indian society and strengthened the rising tide of Indian nationalism. Dyer was censured by the official commission of inquiry but he was hailed as a hero by the 'Anglo-Indians'.

11. K. Natwar-Singh, 'Only Connect . . . Forster and India', *Aspects of Forster*, ed. Oliver Stallybrass (London, 1969), p. 46.

12. Andrew Shonfield, 'The Politics of Forster's India', *Encounter*, 30 (January 1968), 68.

13. Natwar-Singh, p. 43.

14. E. M. Forster, *A Passage to India* (London: Penguin, 1974), p. 108.

15. Forster's keen political sensibility is evident from his non-fictional writings. For instance, his essay on 'The Mind of the Indian State' proves that he could understand very complex political problems.

16. Rudyard Kipling, 'The Education of Otis Yeere', *The Writings in Prose and Verse* (New York, 1897–1936), VI, 9–10.

17. For example notice the primeval Egg of Universe in the Orphic religion: the egg of Night impregnated by the wind and dropped on chaos, from which Eros-Phanes sprang and gave birth to the existing world.

18. Heinrich Zimmer, *Myths and Symbols in Indian Art and Civilisation* (New York, 1946), p. 154.

19. For a full discussion of this point see Benita Parry, *Delusions and Discoveries: Studies on India in the British Imagination, 1880–1930* (London, 1972). Parry is quite right in dismissing W. Stone's thesis (presented in his study *The Cave and the Mountain*, Stanford, California, 1966) that Hinduism offers the key to the mystery of the caves.

20. E. M. Forster, *Abinger Harvest* (Penguin: London, 1976), pp. 293–4.

21. Mohammed Iqbal (1873–1938), who is now known as the philosopher-poet of Pakistan, was one of the most profound writers of twentieth-century India. He was primarily concerned with making Indian Muslims conscious of their Islamic heritage and identity, and he played a leading role in the creation of a separate homeland for Muslims in India. Forster met Iqbal, though very briefly, and in an essay on Iqbal, he declares: 'Mohammed Iqbal is a genius and a commanding one, and though I often disagree with him and usually agree with Tagore, it is Iqbal I would rather read. I know where I am with him. He is one of the two great cultural figures of modern India, and our ignorance about him is extraordinary.' (TC, 295–6)

22. As I stated in the last section, Jainism is a post-Vedic philosophy which is not very far removed from Hindu patterns of belief. Jainism as well as Buddhism are considered unorthodox because they do not acknowledge the *Vedas*. However, the archaic elements in Jainism show that its origin is pre-Hindu.

23. For a fuller treatment of this subject see Larry Collins and Dominique Lapierre, *Freedom at Midnight* (New York, 1975), pp. 153–71.

24. 'E. M. Forster on his Life and Books', *Listener*, 61 (1 January 1959), 11.

25. The term 'Anglo-Indian' was applied originally to all the British in India but was officially adopted in 1900 to describe persons of mixed descent, then known as Eurasians. However, since 'Anglo-Indian' continued to be used in both contexts till the end of the Raj, I have used inverted commas to differentiate between 'Anglo-Indian' (British in India) and Anglo-Indian (person of mixed descent).

26. The Englishwoman (or the *memsahib* as she was called in India) was to a large extent responsible for the breakdown of social contacts between the British and the natives. The *memsahib* never entirely integrated with India; she created her little England wherever she went. Before the Mutiny, things were more relaxed as there were not very many *memsahibs* around, and the Englishmen freely married or had liaisons with native women, which incidentally produced real Anglo-Indians – people of mixed breed.

27. George Orwell, *Burmese Days* (Penguin: London, 1975), p. 17.

28. The controversy over Indian membership, usually presented in terms of a colour-bar, was going strong around the Second World War, and some clubs did admit Indians. See Charles Allen (ed.), *Plain Tales From The Raj* (London, 1975), pp. 99–108.

29. Forster seems to have modelled Fielding after himself and his close friend G. L. Dickinson with whom he first went to India. This impression emerges from Forster's biography of Dickinson where he is portrayed as a humanist who blamed 'Anglo-Indian' haughtiness for the political mess of India. And like

Fielding, Dickinson too did not want to let India go out of the Empire completely. He also believed in good will as a possible solution to the whole issue. However, there are some important differences between Fielding and Dickinson or Forster and Dickinson. For instance, unlike Forster, he felt that the gulf between East and West could not be bridged. See *Goldsworthy Lowes Dickinson* (London, 1934).

30. E. M. Forster, 'Reflections in India: I — Too Late?' *The Nation and the Athenaeum*, 30 (21 January 1922), 201.

31. Santha Rama Rau records Forster telling her that in *A Passage to India* he tried to 'indicate the human predicament in a universe which is not, so far, comprehensible to our minds'. See K. Natwar-Singh (ed.), *E. M. Forster: A Tribute* (London, 1964), p. 50.

CHAPTER 3

1. Thompson's long contact with India, his Wesleyan background, and his later experience as a journalist also connect him with Kipling. There are however many differences. For instance, Thompson's knowledge of India was essentially confined to Hindu Bengal while Kipling was more familiar with Muslim Punjab.

2. Most of the biographical information on Thompson is taken from H. M. Margoliouth's article in *D.N.B. 1941—1950*. I am also greatly indebted to Benita Parry's excellent section on E. J. Thompson; see *Delusions and Discoveries* (London, 1972), pp. 164—202.

3. His perceptive study *Tagore, his Life and Work* (London, 1921) is a proof of his mastery of Bengali poetry.

4. G. T. Garratt (1888—1942) served in the ICS from 1913 to 1923. His primary interest was in history and education; he was principal of Government College, Lahore for some time. Later, he served as political secretary to the Indian Round Table Conferences. He was a close friend of Thompson and shared many of his ideas; see for example his book *An Indian Commentary* (London, 1928).

5. Edward J. Thompson and G. T. Garratt, *Rise and Fulfilment of British Rule in India* (Allahabad, 1962), pp. vii—viii.

6. E. J. Thompson, *A History of India* (London, 1927), pp. 77—8.

7. E. J. Thompson, *The Reconstruction of India* (London, 1930), p. 40.

8. E. J. Thompson, *A Letter from India* (London, 1932), p. 103.

9. In *A Letter from India*, Thompson remarks: 'The Princes, of course, are quite wrong as survivals — in 1940, and their role covers great injustice' (p. 72), and that 'they are the last strongholds in the world anywhere of feudalism and they block Independence' (p. 69).

10. E. J. Thompson, *Enlist India for Freedom!* (London, 1940), p. 10.

11. It is true that Muslim political ranks were divided in the mid-1930s and that the League did not do too well in the 1937 elections. Later on, however, the League became the only true voice of the Indian Muslims who rallied under its banner — the post-1937 events proved this beyond doubt. In March 1940, at their annual meeting in Lahore, the League propounded 'the two nation theory' calling for the creation of Pakistan. The single-minded devotion with which the Muslims of India responded to the call of Pakistan is a fact of history which Thompson tends to ignore.

12. *An Indian Day* (London, 1927) was offered as a 'counterblast' to Forster's *A*

Passage to India though one fails to see the reason for doing so. It is in this partly autobiographical novel (in fact the entire Indian trilogy is autobiographical) that Thompson sets up the familiar locale and characters, especially the educational missionary Alden, his alter ego, through whom he projects his views. Here he attempts to bring out the strength and weaknesses of both Indians and the British with a plea for love and forgiveness which he still thinks can save the Raj. Here the parallel with Forster is obvious. However, the emphasis is on a spiritual plane of understanding rather than political as shown by the transformation of Findlay into a kind of an Indian saint who sees no dichotomy between Hinduism and Christianity. In presenting such a spiritual solution, Thompson is perhaps contradicting the views made in his expository writings.

13. E. J. Thompson, *A Farewell to India* (London, 1931), p. 40.

14. E. J. Thompson, *An Indian Day* (London, 1927), p. 46.

15. For example in *An Indian Day*, this theme is developed through the visit of his sister-in-law to the ancient, ruined city outside Vishnugram where as she contemplates its past, she hears confusing noises (like the echo in Forster's caves) which seem to negate all reality: 'The noises which the generations raise seemed to be nothing – the struggles of insects flung into a sea which is drowning them. The rustle was the eternal voice of the sea itself, the sound which was before man and will be after man has perished. All was unreal, nothing mattered.' (p. 126).

16. E. J. Thompson, *An End of the Hours* (London, 1938), p. 247.

17. Ibid., p. 44.

18. It is interesting to draw some parallels between Alden and Forster's Fielding. In both cases we have a liberal educationist (though Fielding is not a missionary) who abhors racial discrimination and believes in developing friendship with the natives. There are some obvious differences as well. While Fielding rejects imperialism, Alden is a firm supporter of the Raj; he has no sympathy for the national movement. It is, however, Alden's friend Findlay who is finally able to see that friendship with Indians is only possible on a spiritual level and hence is of limited value; this mystical relationship cannot solve the socio-political problems of India. Here the parallel with Mrs Moore comes to the fore.

19. Thompson and Garratt, p. vii.

CHAPTER 4

1. As I mentioned in my 'Introduction', George Orwell, though largely connected with Burma, is in fact writing within the context of the Raj, for at that time Burma was a part of the British Indian Empire.

2. The paradoxical and contradictory nature of Orwell's personality is perhaps the essential factor that lends complexity to his work. For example, Orwell was a rebel with a strong sense of responsibility; he crusaded for a socialistic society, yet he had important reservations about socialism; he knew that socialism implied increased mechanisation, but he had an aversion to modern machinery, and so on. This aspect of Orwell has received considerable scholarly attention. See for instance, Richard J. Voorhees, *The Paradox of George Orwell* (Purdue, 1961).

3. Although, unlike Kipling, Orwell's mother returned to England with him, he lived in residential schools away from home except for summer vacations. He went as a scholarship boy to Wellington and Eton, while Kipling studied at a less exclusive school, United Services College at Westward Ho!

4. Francis Odle, 'Orwell in Burma', *Twentieth Century*, 179 (1972), 38–9.
5. In a letter to Miss Tennyson Jesse, Orwell says that his choice was mainly made because of family ties with Burma. However, the question is that he had more immediate ties with India than with Burma. It is possible that he had to go there because that was the place where a job was secured for him (see for example Jeffrey Meyers's review of Orwell's *Collected Essays, Journalism and Letters* in *Philological Quarterly*, October 1969, 526–33; reprinted in *George Orwell: The Critical Heritage*, ed. Jeffrey Meyers (London, 1975), pp. 373–81). However, I tend to think that a romantic concept of being an empire-builder was the motivating force behind this decision, for Burma, as compared to India, was still virgin ground. Secondly, the police service afforded a greater possibility for a life of action. It may also be noted that the Indian Imperial Police was next in rank and status to the Indian Civil Service; and if one was not ready to go through university and then take the ICS examination, the police was not a bad choice. So I would say that a desire for power, prestige, and action made Orwell choose the police service in Burma.
6. Malcolm Muggeridge, one of Orwell's close friends, recalls that during a meeting in India, Orwell told him that 'Mandalay' was the finest poem in the English language. He also records that at that time Orwell had no liberal tendencies. See *George Orwell: The Critical Heritage*, pp. 359–62.
7. Maung Htin Aung, 'George Orwell and Burma', *The World of George Orwell*, ed. Miriam Gross (London, 1971), pp. 19–30. He also thinks that Orwell went to Burma because of his romantic notions about the role of an empire-builder.
8. Christopher Hollis, *George Orwell* (Chicago, 1956), p. 27.
9. Roger Beadon, 'With Orwell in Burma', *Listener*, 81 (29 May 1969), 755.
10. Malcolm Muggeridge, 'Burmese Days', *World Review*, (June 1950), 45–8. On the points of contact between Orwell and Kipling see also Richard Cook, 'Rudyard Kipling and George Orwell', *Modern Fiction Studies*, 7 (Summer 1961), 125–35.
11. *The Collected Essays, Journalism and Letters of George Orwell*, ed. Sonia Orwell and Ian Angus (Penguin: London, 1975), 4 vols, I, 184. Subsequent references to Orwell's non-fiction, unless otherwise indicated, will be to this edition.
12. Raymond Williams, 'Observation and Imagination in Orwell', *George Orwell: A Collection of Critical Essays*, ed. Raymond Williams (Englewood Cliffs, N.J., 1974), p. 53.
13. During the War Orwell spent two years (1941–3) as Talks Producer for the Indian Section of the BBC, broadcasting anti-Nazi and indirectly pro-British propaganda directed at Indians. Although he never said it in so many words, it amounted to the argument that the Raj was a lesser evil than Russian communism or German fascism. This complacency is further shown in his belief that British propaganda was cleaner than German propaganda; he tried to prove it by including an anti-British talk of Subhas Chandra Bose broadcast from Berlin for comparison along with some BBC talks collected in *Talking to India* (London, 1943). It may also be interesting to note that his assistant was Z. A. Bokhari (who was connected with Government College, Lahore) and his distinguished contributors included E. M. Forster, T. S. Eliot, and Herbert Read.
14. George Orwell, *The Road to Wigan Pier* (Penguin: London, 1976), p. 126.
15. Allen J. Greenberger, *The British Image of India* (London, 1969), pp. 174–6.

16. Orwell's fiction, particularly early fiction, has traditionally been dismissed as a mere polemic on political issues and of slight artistic merit. For example, see John Atkins, *George Orwell* (New York, 1954); Raymond Williams, *George Orwell* (New York, 1971); Maung Htin Aung, 'George Orwell and Burma', *The World of George Orwell*, ed. Miriam Gross (New York, 1971), pp. 10–30. However, recent Orwell scholarship has been much concerned with correcting this view though in its zeal to prove the artistic worth of his fiction, it sometimes goes to the other extreme. See for instance Robert A. Lee, 'Symbol and Structure in *Burmese Days*: A Revaluation', *Texas Studies in Literature and Language*, 11 (1969), 819–35; David L. Kubal, *Outside the Whale: George Orwell's Art and Politics* (Notre Dame, 1972); and John V. Knapp, 'Dance to a Creepy Minuet: Orwell's *Burmese Days*, Precursor of *Animal Farm*', *Modern Fiction Studies*, 21 (1975), 11–30.

17. Jeffrey Meyers, *A Reader's Guide to George Orwell* (London, 1975), pp. 68–9.
18. George Orwell, *Burmese Days* (Penguin: London, 1975), p. 119. Subsequent references will be to this edition.
19. Robert A. Lee, 'Symbol and Structure in *Burmese Days*: A Revaluation', *Texas Studies in Literature and Language*, 11 (1969), 819–35.
20. Maung Htin Aung, 'George Orwell and Burma', *The World of George Orwell*, ed. Miriam Gross (London, 1971), 19–30.
21. David L. Kubal, *Outside the Whale: George Orwell's Art and Politics* (Notre Dame, 1972), pp. 73–4.
22. This was precisely his view on the Raj when he was engaged in anti-Nazi propaganda from the BBC during the Second World War.
23. Quoted by John Atkin, *George Orwell* (New York, 1971), p. 83.
24. E. M. Forster, *Two Cheers for Democracy* (London, 1974), p. 71.

CHAPTER 5

1. John Masters, *Bugles and a Tiger* (New York, 1968), p. 133.
2. Masters accuses Kipling of racism of which he absolves himself completely and makes much ado about his love for India and its peoples. However, it is questionable whether Masters loves Indians or just the Gurkhas. If Kipling dares call his Gurkhas 'Black Infantry', Masters is prepared to call him names: 'Had he meant to speak of Gurkhas in that derogatory sense? If so, he was a color-crazy ass.' (BT, 81) I do not doubt his understanding and fascination for India, but as far as love for Indians is concerned, I am not too sure. He certainly loved his Gurkhas, but Gurkhas are not Indians, a fact which Masters fully understands. On the other hand Kipling's love for Indians is clearly established by *Kim*.
3. The club usually had a billiard room, a dining room, a ballroom, and a library. In the afternoon the card room was filled with women playing bridge and gossiping. The male players usually arrived in the evening, staying till midnight or later. Outside, tennis or squash or swimming facilities were available. It was, however, on the night of the weekly Saturday dance that the club really came to life. (BT, 154)
4. For example an average *memsahib*'s servants included the following: *bhisti* (water carrier), *mehtar* (sweeper), *khansamah* (cook), *masalchi* (dishwasher and assistant cook), *ayah* (children's nurse), and *syce* (groom). Besides these, there were *dhobis* (washermen) who washed and ironed the laundry for about ten rupees a month;

darzis (tailors) who came and set up their machines on the veranda to make dresses and repair clothes; and many others.

5. John Masters, *The Road Past Mandalay* (New York, 1961), p. viii.
6. For example he states:

> Of Gurkhas, what can I say that will compress the knowledge of fourteen years, and all the love and admiration it gave me, into a few sentences? . . . small and sturdy in stature; mountain men all; endowed with an inborn honesty toward life that gives them perfect self-confidence, without any need for swashbuckling or boasting; as fond of pranks as of discipline; cheerful under the worst conditions — especially under the worst conditions; brave, courteous . . . well, you get the idea.
>
> (RM, 8)

7. The immediate cause of the outbreak of the Mutiny was the introduction of the controversial Enfield cartridge that flouted the religious sentiments of both Hindus and Muslims as the cartridge was said to be greased with cow or pig fat.
8. It is true that the British had introduced some good reforms such as abolition of *suttee* or the installation of the railway and the telegraph, but their misdeeds outweighed their deeds. The peasants had been reduced to serfdom through the oppressive land revenue system adopted by the Company. The artisans had lost their trade with the import of British mass-produced goods. The British legal system put the people at the mercy of corrupt courts and deprived them of access to quick and cheap justice. The British schools, colleges, and hospitals seemed to insult their heritage and culture; they appeared to be instruments of conversion to Christianity rather than of education or of treatment. Hence the dissatisfaction against the British rule was genuine and widespread. For leadership people naturally turned to the aged, impotent king of Delhi who still had an appeal, however symbolic, in the idea of a hope of the continuity of their way of life.
9. John Masters, *Nightrunners of Bengal* (New York, 1951), p. vii.
10. Masters suggests that to get a geographical orientation on the story, Bhowani should be imagined to be where Jhansi really is. This further confirms that the Rani of Kishanpur is modelled after the famous Rani of Jhansi.
11. Lakshami Bai, the young widowed Rani of Jhansi, was a heroine of the Mutiny. Jhansi had been annexed by the Company in 1854 in total disregard to earlier treaties. This was deeply resented by both the Rani and her people. At the outbreak of the Mutiny, the Rani was forced into taking control of her state by the sepoys. The British refused to understand her case, holding her responsible for the takeover as well as the killing of the British resident. Sir Hugh Rose besieged Jhansi in March 1857 and the Rani had the choice of either surrendering or fighting it out. She chose the latter course in view of the barbarous record of British occupation. She held out against the superior enemy fighting with skill and courage; she actively guided her troops and regularly attended their drill and training. Her particular interest was in the formation of a force of women. Jhansi was overrun by British troops in April after very heavy fighting. The Rani managed to escape, and she soon joined Tantia Topi and Rao Sahib, two prominent freedom fighters of the time. She participated in a number of compaigns against the British and was finally killed in action at Gwaliar. Sir Hugh Rose called the Rani 'the bravest and best of the military leaders of the

rebels'. See Michael Edwardes, *Red Year: The Indian Rebellion of 1857* (London, 1973), pp. 113–26.

12. Charles Allen (ed.), *Plain Tales From The Raj* (London, 1975), p. 192.
13. See for example Frank Anthony, *Britain's Betrayal in India: The Story of the Anglo-Indian Community* (Delhi, 1969), p. i.
14. John Masters, *Bhowani Junction* (New York, 1954), p. 19.

Bibliography

This list includes all works mentioned in this study and some others that I found useful but had no opportunity to cite directly. However, this is in no way a complete bibliography of material on Anglo-Indian fiction and the Raj.

The place of publication, unless otherwise indicated, is London.

PRIMARY SOURCES (arranged by author)

EDWARD MORGAN FORSTER:

Abinger Harvest, 1936 (refs. to Penguin edn, 1976).
Goldsworthy Lowes Dickinson, 1934.
The Hill of Devi, 1953.
'Indian Entries', *Encounter*, 18 (May–June 1962), 20–7.
A Passage to India, 1924 (refs. to Penguin edn, 1974).
'Reflections in India': I– 'Too Late?' and II– 'The Prince's Progress,' *The Nation and the Athenaeum*, 30 (21 and 28 January 1922), 612–16, 644.
Two Cheers for Democracy, 1951 (refs. to Penguin edn, 1974).

RUDYARD KIPLING:

Rudyard Kipling's Verse, 'Definitive Edition', 1940 (refs. to 1954 edn).
The Writings in Prose and Verse of Rudyard Kipling, 'Outward Bound Edition', 36 vols, New York, 1897–1936.

JOHN MASTERS:

Bhowani Junction, New York, 1954.
Bugles and a Tiger: A Volume of Autobiography, New York, 1956.
Coromandel! 1955.
The Deceivers, 1952.
The Lotus and the Wind, 1953.
Nightrunners of Bengal, New York, 1951.
The Road Past Mandalay, 1961.

To the Coral Strand, 1962.
The Venus of Konpara, 1960.

GEORGE ORWELL:

Burmese Days, 1935 (refs. to Penguin edn, 1975).
The Collected Essays, Journalism and Letters of George Orwell, ed. Sonia
    Orwell and Ian Angus, 4 vols, Penguin, 1968.
Inside the Whale and Other Essays, 1940 (refs. to Penguin edn, 1977).
The Road to Wigan Pier, 1937 (refs. to Penguin edn, 1976).
Shooting an Elephant and Other Essays, 1950.
(ed.), Talking to India, 1943.

EDWARD JOHN THOMPSON:

Atonement: A Play of Modern India in Four Acts, 1924.
Burmese Silver, 1937.
An End of the Hours, 1938.
Enlist India for Freedom! 1940.
Ethical Ideals in India Today, 1942.
A Farewell to India, 1931.
A History of India, 1927.
An Indian Day, 1927.
Introducing the Arnisons, 1935.
A Letter from India, 1932.
The Making of Indian Princes, 1943.
New Recessional and other Poems, 1930.
Night Falls on Siva's Hill, 1931.
The Reconstruction of India, 1930.
(in collaboration with G. T. Garratt), Rise and Fulfilment of British
    Rule in India, 1934.
Suttee: A historical and philosophical enquiry into the Hindu rite of widow-
    burning, 1928.
These Men, thy Friends, 1927.
(in collaboration with Theodosia Thompson), Three Eastern Plays,
    1927.
Thompson Correspondence (with Sir W. Foster and Reginald
    Reynolds), The India Office Library, London.
Thompson–Tagore Correspondence, The Bodleian Library,
    Oxford.
Thompson–Nehru Correspondence, The Nehru Memorial Library,
    New Delhi.

SECONDARY SOURCES

BIBLIOGRAPHIES, THESES, SURVEYS, AND GENERAL WORKS ON
THE IMPERIAL THEME IN LITERATURE AND ANGLO-INDIAN
LITERATURE

Basu, L., *Indian Writers of English Verse*, 1933.
The Commonwealth PEN: An Introduction to the Literature of the British Commonwealth, 1961.
Conybeare, Christopher, *The Role of Empire in English Letters After Kipling*. M.Phil. Thesis. University of London, 1968.
Derrett, M. E., *The Modern Indian Novel in English: A Comparative Approach*, Brussels, 1966.
Garratt, G. T. (ed.), *The Legacy of India*, 1938.
Greenberger, Allan J., *The British Image of India: A Study in the Literature of Imperialism, 1880—1960*, 1969.
Hill, Winifred, *The Overseas Empire in Fiction: An Annotated Bibliography*, 1930.
Howe, Susanne, *Novels of Empire*, New York, 1949.
Iyengar, K. R. S., *The Indian Contribution to English Literature*, Bombay, 1945.
——, *Indian Writing in English*, Bombay, 1962.
——, *Indo-Anglian Literature*, Bombay, 1943.
Journal of Commonwealth Literature, 1965—78.
Meyers, Jeffrey, *Fiction and the Colonial Experience*, 1968.
Mukherjee, Meenakshi, *The Twice Born Fiction*, New Delhi, 1971.
Nicholson, Kai, *A Presentation of Social Problems in the Indo-Anglian & the Anglo-Indian Novel*, Bombay, 1972.
Oaten, Edward Farley, *A Sketch of Anglo-Indian Literature*, 1908.
Parry, Benita, *Delusions and Discoveries: Studies on India in the British Imagination, 1880—1930*, 1972.
Press, John, ed., *Commonwealth Literature: Unity and Diversity in a Common Culture*, 1965.
Raskin, Jonah, *The Mythology of Imperialism: Rudyard Kipling, Joseph Conrad, E. M. Forster, D. H. Lawrence and Joyce Cary*, New York, 1971.
Sencourt, R., *India in English Literature*, 1925.
Sharp, Sir H., *Anglo-Indian Verse*, 1937.
Singh, Bhupal, *A Survey of Anglo-Indian Fiction*, 1934.
Spenser, Dorothy, *A Bibliography: Indian Fiction in English*, University of Pennsylvania, 1960.

Street, Brian V., *The Savage in Literature: Representations of 'Primitive' Society in English Fiction, 1858–1920*, 1975.

Viswanatham, K., *India in English Fiction*, Waltair, India, 1971.

CRITICAL STUDIES (ARRANGED BY AUTHOR)

E. M. Forster

Beer, J., *The Achievement of E. M. Forster*, 1962.

Bradbury, M., ed., *E. M. Forster: A Collection of Critical Essays*, Englewood Cliffs, N. J., 1966.

Brander, Laurence, 'E. M. Forster and India', *A Review of English Literature*, 3 (October 1962), 76–83.

Chaudhuri, Nirad C., 'Passage To and From India', *Encounter*, 2 (June 1954), 19–24.

Cooperman, Stanley, 'The Imperial Posture and The Shrine of Darkness: Kipling's *The Naulahka* and E. M. Forster's *A Passage to India*', *English Literature in Transition*, 6 (1953), 9–13.

Crews, F. C., *E. M. Forster: The Perils of Humanism*, Princeton, 1962.

Das, G. K., *E. M. Forster's India*, 1977.

Daumier, Louise, 'What happened in the Caves? Reflections on *A Passage to India*', *Modern Fiction Studies*, 7 (Autumn 1961), 258–70.

Furbank, P. N., *E. M. Forster: A Life*, 2 vols, 1977–8.

Levine, June Perry, *Creation and Criticism: A Passage To India*, Lincoln, 1971.

McLuhan, H. Marshall, 'Kipling and Forster', *The Sewanee Review*, 52 (1944), 332–43.

Natwar-Singh, K. (ed.), *E. M. Forster: A Tribute*, New York, 1964.

Shahane, V. A. (ed.), *Focus on Forster's A Passage to India: Indian Essays in Criticism*, New Delhi, 1975.

Shonfield, Andrew, 'The Politics of Forster's India', *Encounter*, 30 (January 1968), 62–8.

Stallybrass, Oliver (ed.), *Aspects of Forster*, 1969.

Stone, W., *The Cave and the Mountain: A Study of E. M. Forster*, Stanford, California, 1966.

Thomson, George H., *The Fiction of E. M. Forster*, Detroit, 1967.

Rudyard Kipling

Annan, Noel, 'Rudyard Kipling as a Sociologist', *Kipling Journal*, 111 (October 1954), 5–6.

——, 'Kipling's Place in the History of Ideas', *Victorian Studies*, 3 (June 1960), 323–48.

Carrington, C. E., *Rudyard Kipling: His Life and Work*, 1955.

Cornell, Louis, *Kipling in India*, 1966.

Dobrée, Bonamy, *Rudyard Kipling: Realist and Fabulist*, 1967.

Edwardes, Michael, 'Rudyard Kipling and the Imperial Imagination', *Twentieth Century*, 153 (June 1953), 443–54.

Husain, Syed Sajjad, *Kipling and India*, Dacca, 1965.

Islam, Shamsul, *Kipling's Law: A Study of his Philosophy of Life*, 1975.

Jamiluddin, K., *The Tropic Sun*, Lucknow, 1974.

The Kipling Journal, 1927–78.

Orwell, George, 'Rudyard Kipling', *Horizon*, 5 (February 1942), 111–25.

Rao, K. Bhaskara, *Rudyard Kipling's India*, Oklahoma, 1967.

Rutherford, Andrew (ed.), *Kipling's Mind and Art*, 1964.

Sandison, Alan, *The Wheel of Empire*, 1967.

Shanks, Edward, *Rudyard Kipling: A Study in Literature and Political Ideals*, 1940.

Stevenson, Lionel, 'The Ideas in Kipling's Poetry', *University of Toronto Quarterly*, I (July 1932), 467–89.

Tompkins, J. M. S., *The Art of Rudyard Kipling*, 1959.

Varley, Henry Leland, 'Imperialism and Rudyard Kipling', *Journal of History of Ideas*, 14 (January 1953), 124–35.

Wilson, Angus, *The Strange Ride of Rudyard Kipling: His Life and Works*, 1977.

Wilson, Edmund, 'The Kipling that Nobody Read', *The Wound and the Bow* (Boston, 1941), 105–81.

John Masters

Dempsey, David, 'File on Masters', *New York Times Book Review*, 11 January 1953, 8.

Nichols, Lewis, 'Talk with John Masters', *New York Times Book Review*, 28 March 1954, 15.

'The Soldier's Trade', *Time*, 67 (9 January 1956), 90–2. (Review of *Bugles and a Tiger*.)

George Orwell

Alldritt, Keith, *The Making of George Orwell: An Essay in Literary History*, 1969.

Atkins, John, *George Orwell: A Literary and Biographical Study*, 1954.

Beadon, Roger, 'With Orwell in Burma', *Listener*, 81 (29 May 1969), 755.

Calder, Jenni, *Chronicles of Conscience: A Study of George Orwell and Arthur Koestler*, 1968.

Cook, Richard, 'Rudyard Kipling and George Orwell', *Modern Fiction Studies*, 7 (Summer 1961), 125–35.

Forster, E. M., 'George Orwell', *Two Cheers for Democracy*, New York, 1951.

Greenblatt, Stephen, *Three Modern Satirists: Waugh, Orwell and Huxley*, New Haven, 1965.

Gross, John, 'Imperial Attitudes', *The World of George Orwell*, ed. Miriam Gross (1971), 31–8.

Gross, Miriam (ed.), *The World of George Orwell*, 1971.

Hollis, Christopher, *A Study of George Orwell*, 1956.

Htin Aung, Maung, 'George Orwell and Burma', *Asian Affairs*, 57 (1970), 19–28; reprinted in *The World of George Orwell*, ed. Miriam Gross (1971), 19–30.

——, 'Orwell and the Burma Police', *Asian Affairs*, 60 (1973), 181–6.

Karl, Frederick R., 'George Orwell: The White Man's Burden', *The Contemporary English Novel*, New York, 1965.

Knapp, John, 'Dance to a Creepy Minuet: Orwell's *Burmese Days*', *Modern Fiction Studies*, 21 (1975), 11–29.

Kubal, David L., *Outside the Whale: George Orwell's Art and Politics*, Notre Dame, Indiana, 1972.

Meyers, Geoffrey, *George Orwell: The Critical Heritage*, 1975.

——, *A Reader's Guide to George Orwell*, 1975.

Muggeridge, Malcolm, '*Burmese Days*', *World Review*, 16 (June 1950), 45–8.

——, 'A Knight of the Woeful Countenance', *The World of George Orwell*, ed. Miriam Gross (1971), 165–76.

Odle, Francis, 'Orwell in Burma', *Twentieth Century*, 179 (1972), 38–9.

Oxley, B. T., *George Orwell*, New York, 1969.

Rees, Philip, *George Orwell: Fugitive from the Camp of Victory*, Carbondale, 1961.

Stevens, A. Wilber, 'George Orwell and Southeast Asia', *Yearbook of Comparative and General Literature*, 11 (1962), 133–41.

Trilling, Lionel, 'George Orwell and the Politics of Truth', *The Opposing Self: Nine Essays in Criticism*, 1955.

Voorhees, Richard, *The Paradox of George Orwell*, Lafayette, Indiana, 1961.

Williams, Raymond, *George Orwell*, New York, 1971.

Woodcock, George, *The Crystal Spirit: A Study of George Orwell*, Boston, 1966.

GENERAL WORKS ON COLONIALISM AND INDIA/PAKISTAN (INCLUDING SOME FICTION)

Ali, Yusuf, *A Cultural History of India during the British Period*, Bombay, 1940.

Allan, Charles (ed.), *Plain Tales from the Raj: Images of British India in the Twentieth Century*, 1975.

Allport, Gordon, *The Nature of Prejudice*, Boston, 1954.

Anthony, Frank, *Britain's Betrayal in India: The Story of the Anglo-Indian Community*, Delhi, 1969.

Aziz, K. K., *Britain and Muslim India*, 1963.

Basham, A. L., *The Wonder That Was India*, 1954.

Bennett, George (ed.), *The Concept of Empire: Burke to Attlee, 1774–1947*, 1953.

Besant, Annie, *India: Bond or Free?* New York, 1926.

Blunt, Sir Edward, *The Indian Civil Service*, 1937.

Bodelsen, Carl, *Studies in Mid-Victorian Imperialism*, 1960.

Bolitho, Hector, *Jinnah – the Creator of Pakistan*, 1954.

Brecher, Michael, *Nehru – A Political Biography*, Boston, 1970.

Brown, Hilton, *The Sahibs: The Life and Ways of the British in India as Recorded by Themselves*, 1948.

Buckland, C. E., *Dictionary of Indian Biography*, 1906.

Cameron, James, *An Indian Summer*, 1973.

Caroe, Olaf, *The Pathans*, 1964.

Chamberlain, M. E., *Britain and India: The Interaction of Two Peoples*, Devon, 1974.

Cambridge History of the British Empire, 8 vols, Cambridge, 1929–63.

Chaudhuri, Nirad, C., *The Continent of Circe: An Essay on the Peoples of India*, 1965.

Collins, Larry and Lapierre, Dominique, *Freedom at Midnight*, New York, 1975.

Curtin, Philip D., *Imperialism*, New York, 1971.

Lord Curzon in India: Being a Selection from his Speeches as Viceroy and Governor-General of India, 1898–1905, introduced by Sir Thomas Raleigh, 1906.

Darling, Sir Malcolm, *Apprenticeship to Power: India, 1904–1908,* 1966.

Dickinson, G. L., *An Essay on the Civilization of India, China and Japan,* 1914.

Diver, Maud, *The Englishwoman in India,* 1909.

Dutt, R. Palme, *India Today,* 1940.

Edwardes, Michael, *British India, 1772–1947: A Survey of the Nature and Effects of Alien Rule,* 1967.

——, *Bound to Exile: The Victorians in India,* 1969.

——, *Glorious Sahibs: The Romantic as Empire builder, 1779–1838,* 1969.

——, *The Last Years of British India,* 1964.

——, *Red Year: The Indian Rebellion of 1857,* 1973.

——, *The West in Asia, 1850–1914,* 1967.

Fanon, Frantz, *Black Skin, White Masks,* New York, 1967.

——, *A Dying Colonialism,* New York, 1965.

——, *The Wretched of the Earth,* 1965.

Folz, Robert, *The Concept of Empire in Western Europe from the Fifth to the Fourteenth Century,* trans. Ann Ogilvie, 1969.

Gaikwad, V. R., *The Anglo-Indians,* Bombay, 1967.

Gandhi, Mohandas, *Autobiography,* Boston, 1959.

Garratt, G. T., *An Indian Commentary,* 1928.

Golant, William, *The Long Afternoon: British India, 1601–1947,* 1975.

Griffith, Percival, *British Impact on India,* 1964.

——, *The British In India,* 1946.

Heussler, Robert, *Yesterday's Rulers: The Making of the British Colonial Service,* New York, 1963.

Hudson, H. V., *The Great Divide – Britain, India, Pakistan,* 1969.

Hutchins, Francis G., *The Illusion of Permanence: British Imperialism in India,* Princeton, 1967.

Huttenback, Robert A., *The British Imperial Experience,* New York, 1966.

Kiernan, V. G., *The Lords of Human Kind: European Attitudes Towards the Outside World in the Imperial Age,* 1969.

Kincaid, Dennis, *British Social Life in India, 1608–1937,* 1938.

Knorr, Klaus E., *British Colonial Theories, 1570–1850,* Toronto, 1944.

Latif, Sayid Abdul, *The Influence of English Literature on Urdu Literature,* Calcutta, 1924.

Lawrence, Sir Walter, *The India We Served,* 1928.

Lewis, Martin D. (ed.), *The British in India: Imperialism or Trusteeship?* Boston, 1962.

Lichtheim, George, *Imperialism*, New York, 1971.

Mannoni, O., *Prospero and Caliban: The Psychology of Colonization*, New York, 1956.

Maugham, W. Somerset, *Stories of the East*, New York, 1934.

Mayo, Katherine, *Mother India*, 1927.

McIntyre, W. D., *Colonies into Commonwealth*, 1968.

Mehrotra, S. R., *India and the Commonwealth, 1885–1929*, 1965.

Morris, James, *Pax Britannica: The Climax of an Empire*, 1968.

Morris, John, *Eating the Indian Air: Memories and Present Day Impressions*, 1968.

Mujeeb, M., *The Indian Muslims*, 1967.

Naipaul, V. S., *An Area of Darkness: An Experience of India*, 1964.

Nearing, Scott, *The Twilight of Empire*, New York, 1930.

Nehru, Jawaharlal, *A Bunch of Old Letters Written Mostly to Jawaharlal Nehru and Some Written by Him*, Bombay, 1958.

——, *An Autobiography*, 1936.

——, *The Discovery of India*, New York, 1946.

Nigam, N. K., *Delhi in 1857*, Delhi, 1957.

O'Malley, L. S. S., *The Indian Civil Service*, 1931.

Palmer, J. A. B., *The Mutiny Outbreak at Meerut in 1857*, Cambridge, 1966.

Pannikar, K. M., *Asia and Western Dominance, 1498–1945*, 1953.

Radhakrishnan, S., *Eastern Religions and Western Thought*, Oxford, 1939.

——, *Indian Philosophy*, 1923.

Rawlinson, H., *India: A Short Cultural History*, 1937.

Reed, John R., *Old School Ties: The Public Schools in British Literature*, Syracuse, 1964.

Reynolds, Reginald, *The White Sahibs in India*, 1937.

Sadiq, Muhammed, *A History of Urdu Literature*, 1964.

Sarkar, J., *Economics of British India*, Calcutta, 1917.

Scott, Paul, *The Raj Quartet*; comprising: *The Jewel in the Crown* (1966); *The Day of the Scorpion* (1968); *The Towers of Silence* (1971); *A Division of the Spoils* (1975).

Sears, Stephen W., *The Horizon History of the British Empire*, 1973.

Snyder, Louis (ed.), *The Imperialism Reader*, Princeton, 1962.

Spear, Percival, *The Nabobs: A Study of the Social Life of the English in Eighteenth-Century India*, Oxford, 1963.

——(ed.), *The Oxford History of Modern India, 1740–1947*, Oxford, 1964.

Strachey, John, *The End of Empire*, New York, 1959.

Symonds, Richard, *The British and their Successors: A study in the Development of the Government Services in the New States*, Evanston, 1966.

Thornton, A. P., *Doctrines of Imperialism*, New York, 1965.

——, *For the File on Empire: Essays and Reviews*, 1968.

——, *The Imperial Idea and its Enemies*, 1959.

Tinker, Hugh, *Experiment with Freedom: India and Pakistan*, 1967.

——, *Race, Conflict and the International Order: From Empire to United Nations*, 1977.

Trevelyan, Humphrey, *The India We Left*, 1972.

Tucker, Frank H., *The White Conscience*, New York, 1968.

Wertheim, W. F., *East-West Parallels*, The Hague, 1964.

Woodruff, Philip (pseudonym of Philip Mason).

——,*Call the Next Witness*, 1945.

——, *The Island of Chamba*, 1950.

——, *A Matter of Honour: An Account of the Indian Army*, 1974.

——, *The Men Who Ruled India*, 2 vols, 1953–4.

——, *Patterns of Dominance*, 1970.

——, *The Wild Sweet Witch*, 1947.

Woolf, Leonard, *Diaries in Ceylon, 1908–1911: Records of a Colonial Administrator and Stories from the East*, 1963.

——, *Empire and Commerce in Africa: A Study in Economic Imperialism*, 1920.

——,*Growing: An Autobiography of the Years 1904–1911*, 1961.

——, *Imperialism and Civilization*, 1928.

——, *Sowing: An Autobiography of the Years 1880–1904*, 1960.

——, *The Village in the Jungle*, 1913.

Yule, Henry and A. C. Burnell, *Hobson-Jobson: A Glossary of Anglo-Indian Colloquial Words and Phrases*, 1886; rpt. 1968.

Zimmer, Heinrich, *Myths and Symbols in Indian Arts and Civilization*, ed. Joseph Campbell, New York, 1946; rpt. 1962.

Index